Frames of Mind:
A Post-Jungian Look at Film, Television and Technology

Luke Hockley

For Mary, my wife

Frames of Mind:
A Post-Jungian Look at Film,
Television and Technology

Luke Hockley

intellect Bristol, UK / Chicago, USA

A shorter version of Chapter 1 was previously published as *Cinema as Illusion and Reality,* Spring: A Journal of Archetype and Culture. Vol 73: 2005. ISBN 1-882670-30-2. Chapter 2 was previously published by Harvest: Journal for Jungian Studies. Vol 50: No. 2, 2004. ISSN 0266-4771.

First Published in the UK in 2007 by
Intellect Books, PO Box 862, Bristol BS99 1DE, UK

First published in the USA in 2007 by
Intellect Books, The University of Chicago Press, 1427 E. 60th Street, Chicago, IL 60637, USA

A catalogue record for this book is available from the British Library.

Cover Design: Gabriel Solomons
Copy Editor: Holly Spradling
Typesetting: Mac Style, Nafferton, E. Yorkshire

ISBN 978-1-84150-171-0

Printed and bound by Gutenberg Press, Malta.

CONTENTS

Acknowledgements

Of course, there are too many people to thank for their help and assistance with this project. However, institutionally, it is important to acknowledge the support of the University of Sunderland and, in particular, *The Centre for Research in Media and Cultural Studies*. The International Association for Jungian Studies (IAJS) has offered a productive testing ground for many of the ideas in this book. I wish to thank personally Chris Hauke, for his patience, kind observations and friendship. Our work together on *Chinatown* is contained in Chapter Three. A thank you is owed to the trainees at the C. G. Jung Institute in Zürich who showed me just how divergent and personal the meanings of films can be. Manuel Alvarado must not be forgotten. His unique combination of charm, patience, panic and perseverance has been instrumental in bringing this book into being. To Andrew Samuels and the team at the University of Essex, a big thank you!

Introduction: Analytical Psychology – An Overview

When Jung (1875–1961) comments that '...image alone is the immediate object of knowledge'[1] he makes a claim that is immediately appealing to anyone who wants to understand the meanings that lie in, and behind, films, television programmes and the Internet. For Jung, it is through psychological images that it is possible to come to an understanding of ourselves and of our relationship to the world. As will become clear, these two factors, the individual and his or her cultural location, are inseparable.

That this book adopts a post-Jungian approach might seem to suggest the ideas of analytical psychology are more revealing, or insightful, than those of other schools of psychodynamic thought. This is not necessarily so. However, it is the case that they are less well known, and have been subject to less academic scrutiny and debate. It is also true that analytical psychology offers a rather different perspective to psychoanalysis, not necessarily better but different, raising, as it does, fresh problems and new questions. As Terrie Waddell comments:

> Reading a text through the framework of one primary theorist helps us to more clearly understand the ideas that they are putting forward, and, if appropriate, revise them. With this methodology in mind, analyzing cultural material through psychological approaches is far from analogous to analyzing actual case studies. The body of work left by Jung...might better be understood as a 'tool' that we can use to help us wrestle with meaning. In the academic world the ideas of theorists are rarely taken to be absolutes.[2]

With this lack of absolutes firmly in the foreground it is worth introducing another problem. It was not Jung's intention to refer to, or to write about, the media. He was only tangentially interested in their development. This means in the twenty plus volumes which comprise his collected works there are only a handful of references to the media. Jung wrote from the perspective of a clinical physician. As such his terminology can seem at times a little antiquated, a consequence of being part of what at the time was an emerging subject. Why, then, should Jungian clinical psychology be of use in understanding contemporary mediated communications? One answer is that Jung was fundamentally concerned with the relationship between the individual and his or her environment. Some would see this in developmental terms and in so doing would focus on how the child's early environment affects his or her later development — a point discussed later in this chapter. While not detracting from that argument the suggestion here is that in an image saturated culture, a clinical psychology which has at its very core the importance of 'the image' might have some utility in understanding the role that images play culturally.

Jung's language offers a technical vocabulary and is worth keeping in mind that the points he tries to make are not always immediately obvious. For example, in the following quote, as in much of his writing, Jung refers to psychic activities. To dispense with the obvious, Jung is not referring to supernatural or occult behaviour. Instead he means, rather more straightforwardly, psychological activity.

> We would expect that all psychic activities would produce images of themselves and that this would be their essential nature without which they could not be called 'psychic'. It is difficult to see why unconscious psychic activities should not have the same faculty of producing images as those that are represented by consciousness.[3]

This is an important point. What the term 'image' means in this context is the subject of the next chapter, and to an extent the following one too, but what Jung is suggesting is there is an intrinsic connection between images and unconscious psychological meaning.

Of course, Jung was not the first to suggest that images might have meanings that are not immediately obvious. Freud had done so in his hypotheses about the sexual nature of dream imagery, parapraxis (the so-called Freudian slip) and other momentary lapses in the defences of consciousness. Where Jung differs from his precursors is his insistence on the centrality of the image as a way of understanding the unconscious mechanisms of the psyche. Both Freud's topographic model of the psyche (consciousness, pre-conscious, unconscious) and his later structural model (id, ego, superego) revolved around a view of the psyche in which repression of the unconscious had a central role. The impossibility of the Oedipal situation and the sublimation of sexual libidinal energy is what gave the psyche its dynamic qualities.

Jung adopts a different approach. Like Freud, he suggests that there are essentially three components to the psyche – Consciousness, the Personal Unconscious and the Collective Unconscious (also referred to as the Objective Psyche). Far from repressing the unconscious, Jung's suggestion is that it is vital to bring unconscious contents into consciousness. Repression, or suppression for that matter, as Jung remarks, is as much an option for psychological well-being as beheading is for a headache.[4]

While it is not often put in these terms, this insight now permeates most modern psychotherapy and counseling trainings. The reason that all trainees are required to undertake their own personal therapy is precisely to ensure that their own unconscious concerns do not have an adverse effect on the therapeutic relationship. The unconscious needs to be known, not repressed.

By extension it follows that the unconscious has a potentially positive role to play in individuals' lives. The notion of the unconscious as a positive agency is something of a departure from the Freudian model. Rather than focusing on the need for repression and the inevitability of a fragmented sense of self, Jung's psychological territory is concerned with projection, transference and image formation. These differences are not absolute and Jung's understanding of the dynamics of the psyche allows for repression and fragmentation just as Freud's view encompasses projection and the creation of symbols.

The distinction is one of degree. Freud tended to see the psyche in terms which looked back to childhood, to the universality of the Oedipal complex and the psycho-social requirement to repress such material. By contrast, Jung tends to view the psyche as striving for balance, for health and as essentially forward-looking or teleological. For Jung the psyche behaves just like the rest of the human organism. When hurt the body tries to heal itself. When under attack from infection it defends itself. So too in psychological terms the psyche strives for an optimal homeostatic condition in which its mechanism for self-regulation and balance can function effectively.

Likewise, the biological aging of the body is mirrored by a psychological aging. To this extent Jung's model of the psyche is a developmental one. Here the term 'developmental' refers in a humanistic sense to the maturing of a psychological relationship with the world over time. It is not used to suggest that developments early in childhood affect our later psychology, although this is certainly the case. While Jung was interested in how family dynamics influence later adult life this strand in his work has arguably received something of an undue emphasis, coming mainly from clinical work in the UK, heavily influenced as it was by the ideas of Melanie Klein, and to a lesser extent those of Michael Fordam.

Of more pertinence here is the central notion that while the psyche has an eye to the past, its primary role is to engage the individual in living life to the full and in preparing for the future. As Jung puts it, 'The goal is important only as an idea; the essential thing is the *opus* which leads to the goal: *that* is the goal of a life-time'.[5] Such an engagement with the world means that Jungian psychology has at its very centre the importance of social and cultural factors in shaping our sense of self. In part this is implicit in Jung's constant use of literature, philosophy, science and mythology as sources from which to shed light on contemporary psychological situations, both culturally and personally. More dramatically, Jung remarks: 'Individuation does not shut one out from the world, but gathers the world to oneself.'[6]

The process of individuation, of becoming oneself, is regulated by deep unconscious structures in the psyche. There is a certain ambiguity in Jung's writing about these structures although generally it appears he is assuming some sort of physical and almost biological process. However, Jung also refers to the presence of the structures, which he names 'archetypes' and the role they play, as a hypothesis. Put simply, it is just an explanation that appears to fit the facts as he observed them in his consulting room. It may well be that the reality lies somewhere in-between the two positions. There is a tendency in some branches of Jungian theory to over-literalize the archetypes. This results in treating them as either actual biological structures or as concrete psychological forms. Instead, the archetype is better conceived as a way of understanding, in the form of an image, how an individual is engaging with both inner and outer worlds; it is a type of metaphor which encapsulates, in an emotional manner, what is occurring in the psyche at any given moment.

This said, recent developments in neuroscience seem to be lending some support to the idea that there are neuro-biological structures which serve to regulate our emotional engagement with the world. They appear to be innate and are shaped by an individual's environment and experiences of parenting. A Jungian view of this argument is present by Margaret Wilkinson, in *Coming into Mind* whereas Allan Schore in *Affect, Dysregulation and Disorders of the Self* presents a more general discussion. In any event, as far back as 1954 Jung was quite clear about the interrelationship that existed between innate psychological structures and the development of patterns of behaviour and modes of thought.

> It is in my view a great mistake to suppose that the psyche of new-born child is a *tabula rasa* in the sense that there is absolutely nothing in it. In so far as the child is born with a differentiated brain that is predetermined by heredity and therefore individualized, it meets with sensory stimuli coming from outside not with *any* aptitudes, but with *specific* ones, and this necessarily results in a particular, individual choice and pattern of apperception.[7]

According to Jung, certain patterns appear to occur more regularly than others. It has already been noted that the psyche is essential composed of, and understood through, images. It may therefore come as no surprise that these deep archetypal structures in the psyche make their presence felt through images. Yet a distinction needs to be made between the archetype as a form or structure and the image that it assumes as it mediates between the unconscious and consciousness. While the pattern of the archetype is relatively fixed, its images vary. Jung suggests that the images associated with a given archetypal pattern may be broadly similar even though they will vary over time and will respond to the influences of different cultures and different family experiences.

> The term 'archetype' is often misunderstood as meaning a certain definite mythological image or motif. But this would be no more than a conscious representation, and it would be absurd to assume that such variable representations could be inherited. The archetype is, on the contrary, an inherited *tendency* of the human mind to form representations of mythological motifs – representations that vary a great deal without losing their basic pattern.[8]

Jung imbued these tendencies of the psyche with an almost animistic quality. He thought that images with an archetypal aspect had a quasi-autonomous existence in the psyche. Consequently, as the objective psyche becomes increasing available for conscious introspection so it appears to be populated with splintered fragments of the unconscious self. Jung termed these characters variously the shadow (for the underdeveloped and darker part of the psyche), the anima and animus as the contrasexual elements, the *puer* (child) for the residues of childhood patterns of behaviour carried into adult life, and so on. The emergence of each figure into consciousness is associated with an emotional charge. Put another way, non-rational emotional reactions may indicate the presence of archetypal material when part of the psyche that has not been understood makes its presence felt.

> It is a great mistake in practice to treat an archetype as if it were a mere name, word, or concept. It is far more than that: it is a piece of life, an image connected with the living individual by the bridge of emotion.[9]

These representations are the result of the interaction between archetypal structures and the environment. It therefore follows that the archetypes have something of a mediating role between the objective psyche (also referred to as the collective unconscious) and consciousness. Dreams form one such outlet for this type of imagery but it also is found in other creative activities. Jung encouraged his patients to paint, sculpt and generally play in the knowledge that this would facilitate the movement of unknown psychological material into a form that would be more accessible to our conscious selves. This is also the idea behind 'active imagination' a therapeutic technique where the dreamer imagines themselves inside the dream. S/he takes on the role of individual characters or objects in the dream and in so doing tries to see the dream from their point of view.

Jung was concerned with understanding the role of the individuals in relation to their histories, cultures and social settings. He therefore thought that archetypes could be seen at work in the culture at large, partly in mythological motifs but also in the significant and meaningful events of the day. In his attempt to present a psychological view of cultural and political developments Jung was not always tactful, or accurate. Commentators such as Samuels (*The Political Psyche,* 1993) and Adams (*The Mythological Unconscious,* 2001) have clearly exposed anti-Semitic and racist aspects to some of Jung's writing. Does this mean that the psychology itself is inherently flawed? I think not. However, it is a salutary reminder that in applying psychological methods to cultural material the two aspects need to be in a dialogue. Just as the therapist needs to be in harmony with the client, so too the psychological commentator needs to be attuned to the culture. To assert the primacy of the psychological point of view at the expense of other considerations would be a grave error. In using the framework offered by analytical psychology to explore films, television programmes and the Internet it is important to be mindful that it offers just one perspective on what might be happening. As already noted, insights are always partial.

This turns out to be congruent with Jung's views about the extent to which it is possible to understand the reality of an archetype. Indeed he was keen to stress that the unconscious can never be fully understood. This is partly a problem in logic for if the unconscious were to be fully understood it would have ceased to be unconscious. In his characteristically florid manner Jung comments:

> Not for a moment dare we succumb to the illusion that an archetype can be finally explained and disposed of. Even the best attempts at explanation are only more or less successful translations into another metaphorical language. (Indeed, language itself is only an image.)[10]

As is evident in the above quote, Jung uses a metaphorical terminology as a means to describe and understand unconscious psychological activities. No matter how his writing might appear, Jung is not describing the unconscious in physical terms but rather in terms of its psychical behaviour. Even if analytical psychology's view of the psyche turns out to be compatible with the neuro-scientific view, neuroscience is not going to discover the actual existence of the shadow, the anima and such like. Susan Rowland in *Jung as a Writer*, 2005, makes a similar point as throughout the course of her book she explores in detail how Jung can productively be read in a literary manner. As she notes:

> ...Jung put the expressive creative nature of the psyche *first*. The ability of anyone, including himself, to produce a comprehensive science of the psyche, even to describe psychic processes accurately in worlds, comes second to the innate property of the human mind to be mysterious. Ultimately, the psyche confounds the essentially cultural divisions of science and art, will reveal them to be culture.[11]

Jung terms the process of becoming who you are, in distinction to being content with how your upbringing and culture have fashioned you, individuation. In many ways, on this point at least, Jung's thinking is not so different to Carl Rogers's notion of self-actualization or, indeed, to Winnicott's ideas of the true and false self. What they all share is the idea that somehow individuals get pulled away from their innate sense of who they are and end up living an inauthentic life. Many people pull themselves back onto their 'true' path by themselves, as part of a natural maturation process. Others chose to remain un-individuated, if you will. Another group of people find themselves seemingly at odds with the world. They find it difficult to find a purpose or meaning in life and are stuck with a sense that there is more to life than they experience. For this group one of the outcomes of therapy is to activate the psyche's ability to reconnect itself back to a core sense of self. This might involve exploring where patterns of behaviour have come from, how points of view have been formed and coming to an understanding how systems of belief have been sedimented into the everyday patterns of behaviour. Or course, the techniques of the different psychological orientations are different, as are their technical vocabularies, but much of their intention is the same. Typically, Jung expresses his view on individuation slightly differently at different points in his writing. Sometimes he uses a straightforwardly psychological language, while at other times he is more metaphorical. The following two extracts provide examples of these contrasting styles. 'Individuation means becoming an "in-dividual," and, in so far as "individuality" embraces our innermost, last, and incomparable uniqueness, it also implies becoming one's own self. We could therefore translate individuation as "coming to selfhood" or "self-realization."'[12]

> In so far as this process, as a rule, runs its course unconsciously as it has from time immemorial, it means no more than that the acorn becomes an oak, the calf a cow, and the child and adult. But if the individuation process is made conscious, consciousness must confront the unconscious and a balance between the opposites must be found.[13]

Opposites are important in Analytical Psychology. In the normal way of thinking about opposites each element in the pair is quite separate. Dark and light, left and right, sweet and sour and so forth. But Jung thought that psychologically it was possible for opposites to run into each other so that bringing matters 'up' into consciousness involves going 'down' into the unconscious. He borrowed a term from Heraclitus to describe this type of movement, namely, *enantiodromia*. It therefore follows that opposites in the psyche are not polar opposites, rather they exist on a type of continuum which somehow meets up round the back. The challenge for individuals is to contain what are seemingly contradictory elements.

It therefore comes as no surprise that individuation is not achieved by isolating oneself from the world. Instead, the challenge is to live fully in the world, authentically as the people we truly are. It is for this reason that individuals who have a sense that they do not fit into the world and feel that they are apparently out of step with the way that the majority of people live their lives, may be attracted to analytical psychology. This tying together of the individual and the social also points towards something inherently political in the psychology. While analytical psychology has as yet to fully embrace this possibility, its concern with the intimate details of how individuals live their lives fully in society opens up the possibility to develop a coherent and productive psycho-politics. Indeed it should be noted, that some Jungians might be hostile to this notion, preferring instead to assert the primacy of the unconscious and stressing the importance of the personal and private 'political' work of self-transformation in the consulting room. While not wishing to denigrate this point of view, Jung frequently stressed the importance of cultural factors in the shaping of an individual. In the spirit of *enantiodromia*, presumably the opposite is no less true.

> ...we do not sufficiently distinguish between individualism and individuation. Individualism means deliberately stressing and giving prominence to some supposed peculiarity rather than to collective considerations and obligations. But individuation means precisely the better and more complete fulfillment of the collective quality of the human being...Individuation, therefore, can only mean a process of psychological development that fulfils the individual qualities given; in other words, it is a process by which a [hu]man becomes the definite, unique being he [or she] in fact is.[14]

As Jung succinctly puts it elsewhere, 'One cannot live from anything except what one is'.[15] The difficulty is in coming to know what one is. It is worth noting that this view of the psyche does not pre-suppose a single view about what constitutes mental health. What is right for one person will be anathema to another. Individuation, then, is not about living a 'healthy' life. Such a view would suggest an absolutist view about what constitutes healthy living and normal mental functioning in the world. What concerns Jung is authentic living. The homeostatic model of the psyche he promotes has inbuilt into it enough self-regulation, self-awareness and sense of contradiction and tension to ensure that individuals can engage with the world in a meaningful and productive manner. It does not mean that an individuated person (if such a person exists) would be free from the mental conditions listed in documents such as the American DSM IV (*Psychodynamic Psychiatry in Clinical Practice – The Diagnostic and Statistical Manuel*).

If individuation involves the sifting and integration of personal and collective material, it surely follows that as part of this process individuals need to understand the unique relationship they have to the culture at large. The task is to find a way of making sense of the world, a personal myth if you will. The term myth is a loaded one. For some it has at its root a fundamental desire to deceive. For others myths are a potential source of psychological insight. John Izod summarizes the distinction as follows:

> Myths are not innocent of values. The boldest evidence for that is found in Roland Barthes's Marxist thesis 'Myth Today' (1973). He argued that contemporary myths evacuate history of its factual basis so as to give priority to the connotation that things have always been, and will continue to be, governed by unchanging values...An altogether different perspective has been adopted by Jungians. They see myths as contributing to the regulation and balancing of the psychic system. For them, myths are eloquent expressions of psychological patterns which have healing potential because they can make available to consciousness buried urges, fears and delights...[16]

Rather than viewing competing definitions of 'myth' on alternative sides of a divide, perhaps there is a way that they can be pulled together. This is in keeping with post-Jungian theory, which aims not to establish a lack (as in Freudian and particularly Lacanian theory) but rather to find a productive tension in bringing what might appear to be opposites together. This is the *enantiodromaic* exercise. In this case it shows that myths provide a way for a culture to interpret its history, and to assert that its core values are unchanging. The cultural is passed off as natural and in so doing becomes inherently ideological. Yet it is these same myths which, when deconstructed or, to use a psychological language, made conscious, can expose hidden 'urges, fears and delights'. It is not that myths either hide or expose – they do both. So too our personal myths, our intrinsic beliefs and patterns of behavior help us to integrate with the world, while at the same time they mark out what it is that is unique and distinctive in us. In this sense, our personal pathology and our need for social acceptance go hand in hand.

Izod provides a useful reminder that in understanding films it is important that they are located within their social and cultural contexts. This tried and tested method is central to much of film studies which emphasizes audiences, institutions and the close reading, or interpretation, of films. The aim is to see how meanings move and circulate between the viewers of a film, the film itself, and the imperatives of the large corporations that finance and make the films.

> Looking at the ways in which post-Jungian readings imply that screen myths might work on audiences entails considering how those myths relate to the cultural and ideological values to which the films' audiences were exposed at the time of the product's release. We shall find that questioning the psychological effect of films frequently brings the political context and the intervention of the medium itself into consideration.[17]

Izod's blending of the ideological with psychological is important and welcome. But his project is a strictly academic and intellectual one. His suggestion is that through careful analysis of historical events and situations it might well be possible to take ourselves back to the original conditions in which the film was made. In so doing the film might 'read' very differently, and it is quite possible that its original effects and meaning might be uncovered. Such an exercise is not without merit but it is not the only way to approach uncovering a film's meaning. Understanding the origins of a film is, in some admittedly loose way, analogous to understanding our own origins and how the family environment helps to shape our psychological relationship with the world. But such an intervention is usefully only in so much as it sheds light on the current situation. Childhood is not divorced from adulthood. In the same way, the exploring the 'birth' of a film might tell us something interesting about how our understanding of it has changed over the years and, therefore, what it currently means.

The suggestion is that it is important to hold together the past and the present, and not to succumb to the illusion that somehow intellectual endeavour alone is enough to uncover meaning. Much like an archetype, a film, or any sophisticated media product, evades any attempt to pin it down. Meanings are in state of contestation, shifting and changing. This is not meant to suggest that the function of such polysemic endeavours is to cover a lack, as in the Lacanian view of such matters. Rather, the polysemic nature of such texts is driven by the hermeneutic imperative to make meaning – to make sense of the world. This type of 'sense-making' needs to draw on more than just the resources of thought, it needs the totality of psyche through which to understand and contain the ambiguity of a symbolic, or mythological, relationship to the world.

The argument here is that thinking, feeling, intuiting and sensing are all ways of relating to the world and of arriving at discriminating judgements about the quality of such relationships. In his theory of personality types, Jung identified these elements as core aspects of human characters. As might be expected, while being relatively conscious aspects of personality they also point the way to an inner and less conscious set of dynamics. It is in the interplay between thinking and feeling, between sensing and intuition, that the unconscious makes its presence felt. The unconscious tries to keep the psyche in a state of balance while at the same time ensuring that it is suitably propelled along the path of individuation. At different times, for different people, these elements will coalesce and come together as the unconscious draws to the attention of consciousness what is happening in the psyche.

One of the ways this happens is in dreams. In Freudian dream theory images are essentially the result of the convoluted process of displacement, condensation and visualization. The unconscious process of 'dreamwork' transforms latent content into a more palatable manifest content. Skilful analysis can unpick this work to reveal the true meaning of the dream which will, in some way, reveal the playing out of unconscious Oedipal dynamics. In this model of dream analysis, repression and transformation of culturally unacceptable sexual content takes centre stage. Unlike Freudian dream theory, Jung thought that the function of dreams was to represent what was actually happening in the unconscious. The dream does this in relation to the current psychological situation and undertakes its communication in a way that provides a degree of compensation to the prevailing psychological attitude the dreamer has adopted. He comments:

> I have therefore come to the conclusion that Freud's view that dreams have an essentially wish-fulfilling and sleep-preserving function is too narrow, even though the basic thought of a compensatory biological function is certainly correct....Dreams, I maintain, are compensatory to the conscious situation of the moment.[18]

Later in the same article Jung notes, 'As against Freud's view that the dream is essentially a wish-fulfilment, I hold...that the dream is a *spontaneous self-portrayal, in symbolic form, of the actual situation in the unconscious*'.[19] To an extent films, television programmes and, increasingly, Internet websites capture pockets of this experience in as much as they have the potential to provide an outlet for the expression of unconscious desires and archetypal forms. To be absolutely clear, this is not to say that films, or television programmes, are like dreams. Any more than surfing the Internet is like dreaming, or that dreams are like the cinema. But as visual media they do have elements of communality. Such similarities lie partly in their form and, as Izod notes, partly in the quality of their imagery.

> In common with all cultural forms, films are vehicles for symbolic energy charged not only with collective consciousness but also with shared, irrational material that has its source in the unconscious. Jung used the term 'the collective unconscious' to refer to phenomena that appeared to animate the psychological landscape of the human species; but some post-Jungians have developed the concept of 'the cultural unconscious' which...functions better as an indicator of the provenance of this partially formed energy.[20]

The notion of a cultural unconscious is indeed a controversial one. It seems to perpetuate some of the problems that come from the use of the term 'collective unconscious' rather than the seemingly more neutral 'objective psyche, this is not to suggest that the problem is one only of terminology. The very notion of some sort of unconscious psychological agency is something to which there appears to be an almost instinctive resistance. This is curious as the idea that biologically our bodies operate without the interventions of consciousness is not only easy to accept but also self-evident. Proving altogether more problematic is the suggestion that our interactions with others, and view of ourselves may not be entirely rational and conscious. Another troubling aspect of the 'collective' unconscious is the suggestion that it forms some sort of historical bank of human experience and imagery. Jung seemed to hint at something quite like this. From the post-Jungian perspective the emphasis falls on structure rather than content and on psychological process rather than outcome. It is also helpful to remember that the language in play here is one of hypothesis and metaphor and not one of scientific description. Andrew Samuels flags up some of the issues as follows,

> ...the cultural unconscious as an idea, needs further thought. For example, is the cultural unconscious a kind of repository of cultural experience – a storehouse of difference? Or is it the means, already existing as a potential, by which the human psyche gives birth to cultural difference? Or both?[21]

The focus here, as in much post-Jungian psychology, is on difference. The acceptance and, indeed, containment of difference is at the heart of much of Jung's writing. Much critical psychological writing regards the human condition as essentially structured through a series of 'lacks', of lacunae and of discourses which attempt to paper over such voids. By contrast, the Jungian model of the psyche sees the challenge of making meaning of life as one of holding together differences, of containing the opposites and in so doing acknowledging that this cannot be achieved solely through a one-sidedly rational engagement with the world. It is for this reason that the next two chapters deal with emotions, feelings and what depth psychologies refer to as 'affect'. The intention is to tease out a fuller understanding of how audiences engage with films. In so doing it is possible to see that an audience's relationship with the cinema is not predominantly a rational one.

The first three chapters of this book are concerned with cinema. Chapter One explores the role that fantasy and illusion play in analytical psychology and the extent to which movies depict an outer world or enact an inner psychological reality. The second chapter builds on this theme in exploring why it is that films, which we know to be constructed and artificial, have an enduring emotional appeal and effect. In doing so the focus is on the emotional relationship that viewers have with the screen. The third chapter provides a mini case study. It is an analysis of *Chinatown* (1974), which examines the film's seemingly strange and at times un-natural imagery. It does so to examine why the film activates an unconscious and affective response in its viewers.

The following three chapters are about television. Chapter Four explores how television is watched. It examines the psychological implications of this in terms of the viewers' relationship to the screen, particularly, and contrasts this with how cinema films are seen. The fifth chapter takes the form of an exploration of the psychological relationship between television advertising and narcissistic behaviour. It looks at myths of instantaneous transformation and explores the alchemical imagery that occurs in many advertisements. The final chapter in this triad takes a post-Jungian look at the cultural phenomenon that is *Star Trek*. It suggests that far from offering a utopian view of the future as is often supposed, *Star Trek* has a deeply ambivalent view about the individual value of human existence.

The last two chapters are concerned with technology. Chapter Seven takes a psychological look at the role that communications technology plays in society. In so doing, it attempts to show that while technology is clearly part of the discourse of scientific, rational materialism, it also exists in relation to images of myth, magic, superstition and fantasy. The final chapter explores cultural attitudes towards the Internet and the psychological opportunities it offers for fantasy. In so doing it sees the World Wide Web as a cultural container for both desire and also for anxieties about its possible effects.

To conclude, a word of caution. It is not this book's intention to suggest that somehow in Jung there is an undiscovered, unproblematic set of theories that can shine a brilliant light, thereby illuminating the true nature of the psychological role of mediated imagery in the twenty-first century. Jung's theories and, indeed, his personal life raise many serious questions. They have been extensively debated and documented elsewhere and already alluded to. While such difficulties need to be acknowledged there nonetheless remains at the core of analytical psychology a structural engagement with the world that is revealing. Its focus on the image, however that term is understood, is both important and timely. Equally, some of the theoretical work in film and media studies can bring some clarity to some of Jung's ideas that, at times, can appear a little opaque. Therefore, this needs to be a reciprocal relationship and the remaining chapters in this book will let the ideas of media theory and analytical psychology play off each other, noting similarities where they exist and seeking to contain tension and difference where it is found. As Jung pithily put it, 'Concepts are coined and negotiable values; images are life'.[22]

Notes

1. Jung, C. G. (1954/66) *Collected Works* vol. 16. (London: Routledge and Kegan Paul), para. 201.
2. Waddell, T. *Mis/takes: Archetype, Myth and Identity in Screen Fiction* (Routledge: London, 2006), p. 6.
3. Jung, C. G. (1960/69) *Collected Works* vol. 8. (London: Routledge and Kegan Paul), para. 616.
4. Jung, C. G. (1958/69) *Collected Works* vol. 11. (London: Routledge and Kegan Paul), para. 133.
5. Jung, C. G. (1954/66) *Collected Works* vol. 16. (London: Routledge and Kegan Paul), para. 400. Emphasis as original.
6. Jung, C. G. (1960/69) *Collected Works* vol. 8. (London: Routledge and Kegan Paul), para. 432.
7. Jung, C. G. (1959/68) *Collected Works* vol. 9i. (London: Routledge and Kegan Paul), para. 136. Emphasis as original.
8. Jung, C. G. (1976) *Collected Works* vol. 18. (London: Routledge and Kegan Paul), para. 523. Emphasis as original.
9. *Ibid.*, para. 589.

10. Jung, C. G. (1959/68) *Collected Works* vol. 9i. (London: Routledge and Kegan Paul), para. 271.
11. Rowland, S. *Jung as a Writer*, London: Routledge, 2005, p. 3. Emphasis as original.
12. Jung, C. G. (1953/66) *Collected Works* vol. 7. (London: Routledge and Kegan Paul), para. 266.
13. Jung, C. G. (1958/69) *Collected Works* vol. 11. (London: Routledge and Kegan Paul), para. 755.
14. Jung, C. G. (1953/66) *Collected Works* vol. 7. (London: Routledge and Kegan Paul), para. 267.
15. Jung, C. G. (1963/70) *Collected Works* vol. 14. (London: Routledge and Kegan Paul), para. 310.
16. Izod, J. *Screen, Culture, Psyche. A Post-Jungian Approach to Working with the Audience* (Routledge: London, 2006), pp. 2–3.
17. *Ibid.*, p. 7.
18. Jung, C. G. (1960/69) *Collected Works* vol. 8. (London: Routledge and Kegan Paul), para. 487.
19. *Ibid.*, papa. 505. Emphasis as original.
20. Izod, J. *Screen, Culture, Psyche. A Post-Jungian Approach to Working with the Audience* (Routledge: London, 2006), p. 18.
21. Samuels, A. *The Political Psyche* (Routledge: London. 1993), p. 328.
22. Jung, C. G. (1963/70) *Collected Works*, vol. 14. (London: Routledge & Kegan Paul), para. 226.

1

Cinema as Illusion and Reality

At best, Jung had a somewhat ambivalent attitude to the cinema and indeed the media in general. There are only a handful of references to films in his writing, and most of these are made in interviews with journalists or found in records of group seminars. The main body of the *Collected Works* is virtually devoid of references to movies. Literature and art fare rather better than the cinema and have a whole, if somewhat slender, volume of their own (CW15, *The Spirit of Man in Art and Literature*). However, when Jung did mention cinema he seemed to appreciate the creative potential of the medium. He was particularly impressed by its ability to unlock the unconscious and to represent on-screen what are normally internal psychological processes.

> The movies are far more efficient than the theatre; they are less restricted, they are able to produce amazing symbols to show the collective unconscious, since their methods of presentation are so unlimited.[1]

Jung made this remark somewhere between 1928 and 1930 (it occurs in one of the supplementary volumes to the collected works, *Dream Analysis*) and probably earlier rather than later in that time frame. Almost thirty years later, he seems to have changed his mind as the cinema seems to have fallen out of favour. In an interview with the foreign correspondent for the *Daily Mail* in 1955, Jung comments:

> The strains and stresses of twentieth-century living have so affected the modern mind that in many countries children are no longer able to concentrate. Here in Zürich the schoolteachers of the upper part of the lake asked me why it is that they are no longer able to carry out the full curriculum. The children, they said, seemed unable to concentrate. I told them that the fault lay with the cinema, the radio, television, the continual swish of motor-cars and the drone of planes overhead. For these are all distractions...Worst of all is television.[2]

Jung appears anxious about the pervasive nature of media, and the manner in which they were, and are, consumed. For example, elsewhere in the same interview Jung comments that he has nothing against music, but that he cannot stand background music, particularly if the music is good. He adds that while he can tolerate jazz in the background, Bach deserves to be listened to properly as it is, in his view, music which nurtures the soul. Perhaps the same might also apply to the movies. As such, Jung was not expressing a view about the intrinsic worth of the medium *per se* but rather commenting on the psychological attitude adopted towards it. This is typical of Jung, who tried to stay away from making aesthetic judgements about the artistic merit of a piece of art or literature. Instead, he attempted, with varying degrees of success, to adopt a purely psychological approach as he hoped this would provide further confirmation of his psychological theories. This approach is congruent with the clinical practice he established in which patients were encouraged to paint images from their dreams, not as an aesthetic exercise, but as a way of opening up a psychological dialogue with the unconscious.

While Jung might not have had much to say on the cinema, he certainly seemed to know what he liked. He comments, 'The best movie I ever saw was *The Student of Prague* [1926]. It shows the separation of the conscious man and his shadow, so that the shadow moves by itself'.[3] Elsewhere he remarks:

> The great asset of the movies is the amazing effects they can produce. One sees the man and his reflection in the mirror, and the devil stands behind and beckons to the reflection of the student in the glass, and the reflection comes out in a quite extraordinary way and follows the devil. The student stares into the mirror and can no longer see himself, he is a man without a shadow. And the devil walks away.[4]

Interestingly, Jung made these observations at time when the movies were striving to achieve greater degrees of realism in the way in which they structured their narratives. At that time cinema was still in its infancy. The *Jazz Singer* (1927), the first feature-length film to use synchronized sound, only had a limited number of sequences of dialogue and singing – mostly the sound was courtesy of a Vitaphone Orchestra score. The rules of continuity editing and the conventional processes of film production had yet to be fully embodied within the Hollywood studio system. But what intrigues Jung is not the realist quality of the movies, rather it is the capacity of the cinema to create an illusory, or magical world – a world where shadows can move by themselves and where reflections take on a life of their own.

There are at least two factors at work here which need to be kept in mind in reflecting on Jung's comments. One is his long-standing and pervasive interest in the metaphorical and the other is Jung's passion for the symbolic. While this is conjecture, it may well be that the type of realist cinema which was to become the norm as the Hollywood studio system came to dominate film production, was not as likely to appeal to Jung as the more intense and visually expressive world of early cinema.

Another factor to bear in mind is that much early cinema was based around clearly mythological and psychological themes – *The Student of Prague* is one such film, being in essence a reworking of Faust. It is also in the tradition of German Expressionist film. This film movement is generally taken to refer to films produced between 1919 and 1923, and it encompasses numerous genres including romances, thrillers and fantasy. Visually the films are characterized by dramatic lighting design, with large shadows, stereotypical characters and acting which draws on the stagecraft of the German theatre to create a stylized décor. The result is an almost poetic film language that was ideally suited to the creation of an atmospheric setting.

Jung's interest in the cinema, such as it was, seems to be with its ability to develop what was at the time a new visual and symbolic language that he believed could breathe new life into ancient myths and revitalize them for contemporary times. Perhaps Jung was also intrigued by the magical and phantasmagorical elements of the cinema as he was captivated by illusions that appeared to be real, as is well documented in his interests in spiritualism and mediumistic activities. Indeed, Jung often suggests that the distinction between reality and fantasy is much less clear-cut than is generally assumed in our everyday lives.

> But what is 'illusion'? By what criterion do we judge something to be an illusion? Does anything exist for the psyche that we are entitled to call illusion? What we are pleased to call illusion may be for the psyche an extremely important life-factor, something as indispensable as oxygen for the body – a psychic actuality of overwhelming significance.[5]

In the preceding passage from *The Aims of Psychotherapy* Jung is exploring the nature of the images produced by his patients and, in so doing, he implicitly places the image centre stage as a means by which to understand unconscious processes. He goes on in the article to make the distinction between psychological reality and conscious reality, with the *proviso* that both realities are equally full of illusion. Following this lead, there are two interwoven themes to follow. The first explores the central role that the visual image has in analytical psychology. The second develops these observations in relation to the cinematic experience. In so doing the intention is to suggest why it is that analytical psychology, in distinction to other depth psychologies, is a particularly useful approach in coming to an understanding of how images, and especially films, convey meaning. In so doing, the intention is not to marginalize other approaches. The cinema can usefully be studied and analysed from many different perspectives, but analytical psychology gives an insightful framework through which to explore both the shared and individual meanings of films. It also gives a language through which to articulate the shifting psychological nature of cinematic images, which, on the one hand, are illusory and collective, but which also have the capacity to speak in a relevant and meaningful manner. In fact, how viewers engage with the on-screen fictional worlds of film is unlike any other art form in the way that it blurs the boundaries between the conscious and unconscious aspects of the psyche.

A first step in this process is to remind ourselves that it is a fundamental tenet of analytical psychology that the unconscious and its images are real. A more cautious approach might be to say 'psychologically real', but for Jung what is true for the psyche remains true for life as a whole. This central principle points towards one of Jung's most profound insights, namely that in order to understand the fantasies of patients, their dreams, neuroses, psychoses, auditory and visual hallucinations and such like, the 'delusions' must be accepted as real. His premise was that as they were real for the patients, for therapeutic purposes the analyst should also take them as real. For Jung, the realms of imagination and fantasy were part of the fabric of the material world. This will prove important in coming to a view about the psychological relationship audiences have with movies and the cinematic experience more generally. The blurring of the divisions between real and not real, between conscious and the unconscious, between the personal and the collective, will be of central concern since images facilitate the merging of what typically are regarded as separate realms.

It is important to be clear here about what Jung means by the term 'image'. This is not as straightforward as might be imagined. For Jung, the image exists somewhere in the space between the unconscious and consciousness. The image is not fully vested with the influence of the unconscious because this would mean that it could be mistaken as something actual or concrete – that is the prerogative of hallucinations. Rather, it serves as a mediator between unconscious contents and outer reality. He describes it as follows:

> When I speak of 'image' in this book, I do not mean the psychic reflection of an external object, but a concept derived from poetic usage, namely, a figure of fancy of *fantasy-image*, which is related only indirectly to the perception of an external object. This image depends much more on unconscious fantasy activity, and as the product of such activity it appears more or less abruptly in consciousness, somewhat in the manner of a vision or hallucination, but without possessing the morbid traits that are found in a clinical picture. The image has the psychological character of a fantasy idea and never the quasi-real character of an hallucination, ie., it never takes the place of reality, and can always be distinguished from sensuous reality by the fact that it is an 'inner' image.[6]

It therefore follows that such images need not be pictorial; rather they are metaphorical, like the image 'heard' in a piece of music. A psychological film theory needs to be concerned with both types of images. More explicitly, the interest rests on the interplay between the overtly audio-visual experience of films and their capacity to both awaken and to be part of our inner lives. In other words, the image exists not just on the screen but also somewhere in the space between the viewer and the screen. Interestingly, this view is consistent with the observation of Roland Barthes in his article *Death of the Author* (1977) in which he outlined his view that meanings come not just from the text, but also from what the reader brings to the text. In the case of the cinema, this may be an unconscious fantasy-orientated process in which the individual plays a role in creating an image – a unique psychosomatic relationship of conscious and unconscious processes activated by the progression of images and sounds on the screen.

Jung maintained that images are central to the construction of the psyche. The innate capacity of humankind to make images is for him what forms the substratum of psychological life. In turn these images refer us back to the deep structures of the unconscious which Jung termed archetypes. These are the patterns which influence our psychological development and growth. They are also the patterns that interact with our culture, our personal experiences and family lives to bring shape and form to an individual psyche. The archetypes are the mechanism through which the psyche maintains its sense of balance and health. Compensating for any disruption to the natural state of the psyche, they ensure that the whole person, mind and body, stays healthy. In so doing they have a crucial role to play in guiding each individual on the quest for wholeness which Jung termed 'individuation'.

The archetypes make their presence known in a variety of ways: they find their way into our dreams; they can alter our behaviour, physical and psychological. Such archetypal behaviour can suddenly escape from the unconscious when individuals are under pressure, or threatened and then they find themselves behaving in ways that they do not understand or are 'out of character'. The affective power of the archetypes is experienced at the important moments of our life, at births, deaths, marriages and other occasions where the spontaneous outpouring of uncontrollable emotion tells us that this is unconscious material. However, and significantly, it is possible to come to know and recognize these archetypes through images, and these images belong at the same time to the inner world and the outer world. Put another way, the psyche is image.

> ...the psyche consists essentially of images. It is a series of images in the truest sense, not an accidental juxtaposition or sequence, but a structure that is throughout full of meaning and purpose; it is a 'picturing' of vital activities. And just as the material of the body that is ready for life has need of the psyche in order to be capable of life, so the psyche presupposes the living body in order that its images may live.[7]

The structure to which Jung alludes in the preceding quote is the structural make-up of the archetypes within the unconscious. He is at pains to note that these structures have meaning and purpose and put individuals in touch with their inner selves; they act as guides assisting in the realization that aspects of unconscious life can effect and affect our everyday relationships and engagement with the world. As such the image captures the psychological reality of a given situation and encapsulate the complex dynamics that arise from the interplay of archetypal forces and their relationship with consciousness as it tries to come to an informed understanding of what is at hand.

> The inner image is a complex structure made up of the most varied material from the most varied sources. It is no conglomerate, however, but a homogeneous product with a meaning of its own. The image is a *condensed expression of the psychic situation as a whole*, and not merely, nor even predominately, of unconscious contents pure and simple...Accordingly the image is an expression of the unconscious as well as the conscious situation of the moment. The interpretation of its meaning, therefore, can start neither from the conscious alone nor from the unconscious alone, but only from their reciprocal relationship.[8]

This is, as Jung puts it, a 'vital activity' as the drive within each one of us towards individuation requires us to understand the complexities of the contradictions that are housed within each one of us. In his book *Re-Visioning Psychology* James Hillman develops this theme:

> Since we can know only fantasy-images directly and immediately, and from these images create our worlds and call them realities, we live in a world that is neither 'inner' nor 'outer'. Rather the psychic world is an imaginal world, just as image is psyche. Paradoxically, at the same time these images are in us and we live in the midst of them. The psychic world is experienced empirically as inside us and yet it encompasses us with images.[9]

The important points to focus on are firstly that the psyche is imagistic and secondly that these images are both inner and outer, *at the same time*. At first this may sound a little confusing and to shed some light on the situation it is necessary to understand what Jung means by the term 'projection'. For Jung, the projection of unconscious material happens not as a defence mechanism but as something over which there is little control. It is the psyche's way of taking a complex (an unresolved psychological problem) and bringing it to the attention of consciousness. When the reaction to a person or situation is under the influence of a projection, it as though the complex belongs to the other person – as though this is all to do with the other. These reactions often carry a disproportionate emotional charge with them – indeed this is one of the ways they can be recognized. For example, it might be worth reflecting on why someone takes such an instant and deep-rooted dislike to someone whom they have just been introduced. Something annoying about another person can turn out to be instrumental in revealing something about ourselves. Interestingly, viewers make similar psychological judgements about the films they watch. They actively seek out films that they think they will enjoy or, to use a more psychological language, which will bring them pleasure. There is an almost sensuous and erotic engagement in the richness and vicissitudes of the visual and aural overindulgence of the cinematic spectacle. Of course, sometimes a film is almost 'stumbled upon' to which there is a strong emotional reaction. Even though this is unintended it is almost as though the psyche is purposeful enough to synchronistically steer us towards the type of film that is needed in a given moment.

Complexes can be positive as well as negative. A positive complex is at work when something is fascinating, when there is seemingly no option but to find out more. It is a special sort of falling in love, with a person, place or idea. It is only later that it is possible to dissolve the projection and to realize that what provided the attraction was an unrecognized sense of one of our best qualities. Alternatively it may be that the quality is latent in an individual, and unconsciously s/he is drawn towards it, as now is the time for it to be developed and integrated into everyday life.

Likewise films can be both appealing and unappealing, and it is quite normal to find them boring, dull, stupid, enthralling, banal, sensual, pornographic, moving, violent, too violent, exciting, child-like, insightful. These represent careful astute psychological judgements. On the one hand, these views may represent accurate clear judgements about a film, but they are also personal subjective evaluations which are based on psychological needs. This would go some way to explaining why it is that the same film can be deeply loved by one person but without value for someone else. Perhaps the most likely explanation is that our views of films are both objective and subjective, conscious and unconscious, and the imagistic environment of the cinema encourages such reciprocity and interplay.

Of course there are many different ways and motivations for watching a movie and viewers will have their own reason for going to the cinema. It might be romantic, it might be to keep the kids quiet – the psychological reason for going is only one of many, but cinema-going can be a profoundly psychological process, and one that has therapeutic outcome. Indeed, it may be that the apparent (conscious) reason for going to the movies acts as a cover for the real underlying motivation.

Watching films in the cinema is not the same as watching them at home, even though there is a current trend to attempt to recreate the cinema experience at home, with large screens and surround sound. This is not the place to get diverted into suggestions that the cinema is womb-like, dark, warm and safe. Nor that it is bed-like, relaxed, comfortable, with the lights low. It is, of course, a little like all these things, but it is equally not like them and they are not the most significant factors in a viewer's relationship with the cinema screen. What is clear is that there is a physical quality to the cinematic experience. The sheer size of the screen and weight of the sound make watching a film in the cinema a physical, bodily, somatic experience. The immersive quality of the environment helps viewers to make the transition from the here and now, into the fictional world of the film. Cinema-going is a psychosomatic experience – something that affects viewers on both bodily and psychological planes, even the most dedicated filmgoers can find themselves surprised at their uncontrollable physical reactions.

Another central part of watching a movie in the cinema is that it is a collective experience. Individual viewers will have a personal experience of a film, but at the same time it is a collective one. This leads to the strange phenomenon whereby screenings of a film have a different quality or atmosphere. I vividly remember co-hosting a seminar with a Jungian analyst at the C G Jung Institute in Zürich. We were doing some work on how films can awaken emotional responses. As is normal practice we showed a number of extracts. One was from a film I knew very well, but it was not a sequence which had any particular personal meaning for me – if anything, I find it a little overly sentimental. However, on that occasion the atmosphere grew heavy in the room, it was almost as though there was a weight pressing down, and I and felt the collective emotion sink into my gut. We took a break. Somehow, at that moment, for that group something happened – there was a sense of what Jung termed the *participation mystique* in which personal and collective identities momentarily fuse.

Another way of describing this situation is as a 'fantasy'. Jung suggests that these fantasies occur independently of consciousness but in relation to it. It follows from this that unconscious fantasies may incorporate real people, real events and actual memories. However, since conscious experiences are not directly related to the fantasy, it becomes important to distinguish between the projection of the fantasy onto real people and events and the fantasy itself. As Jung puts it:

> The psyche creates reality every day. The only expression I can use for this activity is *fantasy*. Fantasy is just as much feeling as thinking; as much intuition as sensation. There is no psychic function that, through fantasy, is not inextricably bound up with the other psychic functions. Sometimes it appears in primordial form, sometimes it is the ultimate and boldest product of all our faculties combined. Fantasy, therefore, seems to me the clearest expression of the specific activity of the psyche. It is, pre-eminently, the creative activity from which the answers to all answerable questions come; it is the mother of all possibilities, where, like all psychological opposites, the inner and outer worlds are joined together in living union.[10]

It is, therefore, clear that fantasy is not in and of itself pathological. In fact, quite the opposite is true, as fantasy is integral to living life in a creative and fulfilling manner. But in order for this to happen, consciousness must be able to discriminate between what belongs to the unconscious and what has been, and can be, integrated into consciousness. Thus, the fantasy manifests itself in the form of image that contains both unconscious and conscious elements, and, in so doing, it forms a bridge between inner and outer worlds. However, to derive benefit from the image, any projections must be withdrawn and, in so doing, consciousness (some might say ego-consciousness) gains a better purchase on the reality of a given situation.

Jung terms this ability to hold together opposing views of a situation the transcendent function, and it enables the psyche to move from one psychological approach, or attitude, to another. Such an approach can be regarded as transcendent in as much as it enables the individual to 'see', or be aware of, the competing 'push' of the unconscious and 'pull' of consciousness. The result is the ability to contain these differing perspectives and, in so doing, to 'transcend' what would otherwise be a purely instinctual response to a situation. The transcendent function is the mechanism by which the psyche gains fuller insight into how our unconscious selves influence our engagement with the outer world in symbolic form.

Here there is a clear difference in terminology between psychoanalytic language and that used by analytical psychology. For Freud, the symbol was a sign or symptom of a repressed idea or wish, normally sexual in origin. By contrast, Jung sees the symbol as something that depicts the psychological reality of a situation as it is, or will be. As such, the symbol has a quasi-allegorical role in depicting and mediating between conscious and unconscious elements – it is expressive of the tensions that are inherent aspects of the transcendent function.

As mentioned earlier, underpinning all these activities is the fact that the psyche has a propensity towards growth. As such, there is a teleological imperative behind its activities, which constitutes what Jung refers to as the process of individuation. This involves each individual becoming who they are and fully aware of themselves and their interactions with others. As such it should not be confused with individualization, for the process of individuation involves becoming ever more responsible for our social and collective relationships – to fully relate to others we must be fully aware of ourselves.

The following quote from Jung neatly summarizes much of the preceding discussion and highlights the natural and creative role that fantasy plays for the psyche in resolving neuroses and in ensuring that the psyche is regulated and healthy.

> If, as in this book, fantasy is taken for what it is – a natural expression of life which we can at most seek to understand but cannot correct – it will yield possibilities of psychic development that are of utmost importance for the cure of psychogenic neuroses and of the milder psychotic disturbances. Fantasies should not be negatively valued by subjecting them to rationalistic prejudices; they also have a positive aspect as creative compensations of the conscious attitude, which is always in danger of incompleteness and one-sidedness. Fantasy is a self-justifying biological function, and the question of its practical use arises only when it has to be channelled into so-called concrete reality...Fantasy is the natural life of the psyche, which at the same time harbours in itself the irrational creative factor.[11]

Cinema has the capacity to draw us into fictional worlds that become momentarily almost real. These worlds are collective (in both the social and psychological senses of the term) and personal. What we experience in the cinema is an awakening of personal and collective psychological material, which mirrors the way in which images behave in the psyche. It therefore follows that it is possible to derive psychological benefit from many different types of films and not just good, high-art, worthy films. In *The Dream and the Underworld* (1979), Hillman refers to 'the polymorphous and pornographic desires of the psyche, refer[ing] to the underworld of images'.[12] Making a similar point, Jung uses an alchemical image to show that what might appear to be without meaning may, actually, turn out to be important.

> Like this apprentice, [alchemist's apprentice] the modern man begins with an unseemly *prima materia* which presents itself in unexpected form – a contemptible fantasy which, like the stone that the builders rejected, is 'flung into the street' and is so 'cheap' that people do not even look at it. He will observe it from day to day and note its alternations until his eyes are opened...The light that gradually dawns on him consists in his understanding that fantasy is a real psychic process which is happening to him personally.[13]

It may well be that the most unlikely of movies, the most contemptible fantasies, the least palatable to our aesthetic and conscious-focused senses, actually capture some of the desires of the unconscious. Zombie movies, where the dead come back to life but only as destructive soulless bodies; vampire movies where the dark sexual stranger kills or incarcerates you in a body that needs fresh human blood to stay alive; the paranoia of the guilty secret coming to light; overt eroticism; enjoying the spectacle of death, all are regularly experienced in the cinema. Indeed, much of this is bound up with genre expectations, which lead viewers to express strong preferences one way or the other not just about individual films, but a whole genre. Significantly, these are not just aesthetic judgements but also psychological ones.

 While he was not writing about films *per se*, Hillman in *Re-Visioning Psychology* (1977) suggests that it is in such pathologized images that the most potential for transformation is found.

> Thus the most distressing images in dreams and fantasies, those we shy from for their disgusting distortion and perversion, are precisely the ones that break the allegorical frame of what we think we know about this person or that, this trait of ourselves or that. The 'worst' images are thus the best, for they are the ones that restore a figure to its pristine power as a numinous person at work in the soul.[14]

As images unfold in front of us, watching them can require us to undertake a 'heroic' activity, while inner and outer, collective and personal, light and dark, the real and the illusory, temporarily coexist and have to be contained within our own experience of the moment. The psychological insight which analytical psychology offers, is that when the term image is used to describe the cinematic experience which occurs, it actually encompasses the image on screen, our physical reactions, and our conscious and unconscious engagement in the process. As the images and sound on the screen pass frame by frame, so too do these other psychological and metaphorical images.

The mythological analogue to this cinematic experience can be expressed in numerous images. For example, there is the alchemic vessel within which the *prima materia* is transformed; alternatively, there is the bright rectangle of moving light, which is differentiated from the still darkness of the auditorium. At risk of an overly inflated image, each screening of a film is a miniature act of creation, as something comes into being which requires viewers to engage with its contents – to come to terms with what is found in the darkness.

> The hero's main feat is to overcome the monster of darkness: it is the long-hoped-for and expected triumph of consciousness over the unconscious…The coming of consciousness was probably the most tremendous experience of primeval times, for with it a world came into being whose existence no one had suspected before. 'And God said, "Let there be light!"' is the projection of the immemorial experience of the separation of consciousness from the unconscious.[15]

Perhaps there is a benefit in just being exposed to movies and there is something satisfying in the physical and psychological aspects of watching a film – identifying with the characters on-screen as viewers encounter the embodiment of fragmented parts of themselves and recognize similarities and differences. Experiencing opposites (what is not like me) is one way of noticing similarities, and in part movies can be used as a type of imagistic transitional object, as a transformative space in which to experience aspects of our psyche. Put differently, Hillman writes about the importance of adopting an underworld perspective that, '...takes the image as all there is'.[16] The suggestion is that immersion in the unconscious act and state of image making is enough, since the psyche needs to experience itself as image, as metaphor, and to comprehend its own interior image-based relationships. Later in the same piece, he adds, 'It is better to keep the dream's black dog [image] before your sense all day than to "know" its meaning...Interpretation arises when we have lost touch with the images...'.[17] But this immersion, the loss of discrimination and conscious engagement, is worrying. Perhaps there is more:

> 'Reflection' should be understood not simply as an act of thought, but rather as an attitude. It is a privilege born of human freedom in contradistinction to the compulsion of natural law. As the word itself testifies ('reflection' means literally 'bending back'), reflection is a spiritual act that runs counter to the natural process; an act whereby we stop, call something to mind, form a picture, and take up a relation to and come to terms with what we have seen. It should, therefore, be understood as an act of *becoming conscious*.[18]

To this extent, if viewers are to derive the maximum psychological benefit from a film as viewers they need to question. Mirroring what physically happens as light is shone onto the screen, this process is one that involves both projection and reflection – it is one that involves an ongoing process of seeing and recognizing. Using language that is reminiscent of the viewer's relationship to the cinema screen, Jung puts it like this:

> This recognition is absolutely necessary and marks an important advance. So long as he simply looks at the pictures he is like the foolish Parsifal, who forgot to ask the vital question because he was not aware of his participation in the action. Then, if the flow of images ceases, next to nothing has happened even though the process is repeated a thousand times. But if you recognise your own involvement you yourself must enter into the process with your personal reactions, just as if you were one of the fantasy figures, or rather, as if the drama being enacted before your eyes were real. It is a psychic fact that this fantasy is happening, and it was really as you – as a psychic entity – are real.[19]*

It therefore follows that the therapeutic aspect (the viewer-as-therapist, if you will) really comes into play when we start to ask 'Why?' Why do I find this film boring? Why am I, for example, repelled by its explicit sexual imagery? Is it down to my politics, or my psyche, or is it more likely the interplay between the two? Why do I feel this? What does it tell me about myself and what I am going to do? Films can activate 'complex' (and the term is used advisedly) material. Adopting a psychological approach to film, it is possible for viewers to work with their experiences. They can pay attention not just to their psychological reactions, to what is seen, but also to bodily responses; crying, cringing, holding someone's hand for comfort, it may even be impossible to stay in the cinema. Crucially, these reactions are taken with us long after the cinema has been left. Then it is possible to test personal reactions to the film with those of our friends or partners as by reflecting on what was seen.

The uniqueness of the psyche can never enter wholly into reality, it can only be realised approximately, though it still remains the absolute basis of all consciousness. The deeper 'layers' of the psyche lose their individual uniqueness as they retreat farther and farther into darkness. 'Lower down,' that is to say as they approach the autonomous functional systems, they become increasingly collective until they are universalised and extinguished in the body's materiality, i.e., in chemical substances. The body's carbon is simply carbon. Hence 'at bottom' the psyche is simply 'world'.[20]

This chapter has tried to present a post-Jungian view of what is meant by the term 'image'. In so doing, it has adopted a view of the cinematic experience that locates the viewer and film as co-protagonists in the process of constructing meaning through the act of image making. The next chapter explores why the reasons for engaging in this type of activity and is particularly concerned with the emotional and affect-driven responses viewers have while watching films.

Notes

1. Seminar Papers, part. 1. *Dream Analysis: Notes of the Seminar given in 1928–1930*, edited McGuire, W., (London: Routledge, 1984), p. 12.
2. Jung, C. G. *Jung Speaking: Interviews and Encounters*. Eds. McGuire and Hull. (London: Picador, 1980), pp. 240–241. (Edited version of interview given to Frederick Sands, foreign correspondent for the London *Daily Mail*, 25–29 April, 1955.)
3. Seminar Papers, vol. 1. *Dream Analysis: Notes of the Seminar given in 1928–1930*, edited McGuire, W., (London: Routledge, 1984), p. 259.
4. *Ibid.*, pp. 49–50. It is worth pointing out that there is an earlier version of *The Student of Prague* from 1913, directed by Stellan Rye that also contains the same scene, but it seems likely that it was the 1926 version that Jung has seen. Whichever version it was, the general psychological points hold good.
5. Jung, C. G. (1954/66) *Collected Works* vol. 16. (London: Routledge and Kegan Paul), para. 111.
6. Jung, C. G. (1964/71) *Collected Works*, vol. 6. (London: Routledge and Kegan Paul), para. 743. Emphasis as original.
7. Jung, C. G. (1960/69) *Collected Works* vol. 8. (London: Routledge and Kegan Paul), para. 618.
8. Jung, C. G. (1964/71) *Collected Works* vol. 6. (London: Routledge and Kegan Paul), para. 745. Emphasis as original.
9. Hillman, J. *Re-Visioning Psychology*. (New York: Harper and Row, 1977), p. 23.
10. Jung, C. G. (1964/71) *Collected Works*, vol. 6. (London: Routledge and Kegan Paul), para. 78. Emphasis as original.
11. Jung, C. G. (1976) *Collected Works* vol.18. (London: Routledge and Kegan Paul), para. 1249.
12. Hillman, J. *The Dream and the Underworld*, (New York: Harper and Row, 1979), p. 45.
13. Jung, C. G. (1963/70) *Collected Works*, vol.14. (London: Routledge and Kegan Paul), para. 752–3. Jung may be referring to the passage which occurs in all the synoptic gospels where Jesus asks: 'Have you not read this scripture: "The stone

that the builders rejected has become the cornerstone [or keystone]; this was the Lord's doing, and it is amazing in our eyes"?' Mark 12:10–11, also Matthew 21:42 and Luke 20:17–18. The passage of scripture that Jesus is referring to is Psalm 118, 22–23. He does so in order to suggest that in fact he is the overlooked keystone (the son of God), a claim which does not sit well with the scribes and chief priest who realize that this parable is being told against them.

14. Hillman, J. *Re-Visioning Psychology*. (New York: Harper and Row, 1977), p. 8.
15. Jung, C. G. (1959/68) *Collected Works* vol. 9i. (London: Routledge and Kegan Paul), para. 284.
16. Hillman, J. *The Dream and the Underworld*, (New York: Harper and Row, 1979), p. 80.
17. *Ibid.*, pp. 122–123.
18. Jung, C. G. (1958/69) *Collected Works* vol.11. (London: Routledge and Kegan Paul), para. 235n. Emphasis as original.
19. Jung, C. G. (1963/70) *Collected Works* vol.14. (London: Routledge and Kegan Paul), para. 753.
    *According to the version of the story by Chrétien de Troyes, *Perceval* (Parsifal) is told by his cousin Sigune that on seeing 'a lance whose tip bleeds without there being any flesh or vein there' he should have asked 'why it bled?'. On seeing the grail and its attendants he should have enquired, 'where they were going like this?". (Lines 3543–3586) Failing to ask these questions she renames him, 'Perceval the wretched!'. For asking the questions 'would have brought such benefit to the good king who is crippled that he would have completely regained the use of his limbs and governed his land; and from that you would have reaped such profit! But now you may be sure that many misfortunes will befall you and others'.
20. Jung, C. G. (1959/68) *The Collected Works*, vol.9i. (London: Routledge and Kegan Paul), para. 291.

2

Watching Films: The Affective Power of Cinema

Introduction

At risk of stating the obvious, going to the cinema can be an emotional and moving experience. It is clear from our own reactions, and from the rest of the audience, that films can awaken deep feelings and emotions. As mentioned in the preceding chapter, the collective nature of the experience can even lead to the odd sense that some screenings of films are better than others. It seems there are occasions when the film can move us more than at other times. It is almost as if there is something transitory or momentary bound up in the nature of the cinematic experience. The darkened auditorium, the large screen and the immersive surround sound all help to make the cinema a particularly intense and rich emotional environment; all assist in focusing our attention on the unfolding drama. Our sense of who we are and what we are doing is temporarily dissolved by, and into, the flow of cinematic images and sounds as viewers are momentarily stitched into the story – *sutured* by, and into, the on-screen diegesis that is the momentarily believable world of the fiction film. But such knowledge does not help to understand why it is that we care about the characters we see on the screen in front of us. This makes the real emotions that we experience all the more puzzling.

Given the power of cinema films to awaken such responses it is curious that academic film theory has paid virtually no attention to the issue of the emotional relationship that viewers have with films. In fact, it is not unreasonable to suggest that the topic of emotions is positively avoided and when they do make an appearance, film theorists tend to present them as if they were in someway undesirable. The following quote is from Herbert Schiller's work on special effects. As a cultural commentator with a particular interest in the economics of the cultural industries he derides the burgeoning of the special effects film industry. He comments: 'Special effects sound and imagery short circuit the brain and hit the gut. Content recedes and reflection disappears as technique flourishes. This may be the defining feature of what is called postmodernity.'[1]

Leaving aside Schiller's claim about the nature of postmodernity (which makes little sense), what is interesting is the linkage he makes between something that can 'hit the gut', and the erosion of content; the suspicion is that something which evokes such emotions cannot be wholesome. Later this chapter explores how this ethos has ended up inscribed into the rhetoric of film studies. Needless to say, the view offered by analytical psychology offers a much needed counter to this approach. It will explore why rationality and emotion have equally important roles to play as parts of the cinematic experience.

It may not have escaped the reader's notice that even though this chapter is ostensibly about affect, that so far the term has not been used – instead it has been concerned with emotions. The reason for this is that in much Jungian literature the terms emotion and affect are used interchangeably; they are, quite simply, synonyms – a point that will be returned to below. Freudian psychoanalytic theory is more circumscribed in its terminology and the end of this piece will explore if Jungian theory might be able to gain something from paying this sort of attention to its technical vocabulary.

In the meantime it is important to remember the distinction that Jungian theory makes between emotions/affect and feelings. One of the clearest formulations of this is found in Jung's work on the theory of personality type. Here he identified four functions: *sensation*, which tells us that something is; *thinking*, which tells us about the thing; *intuition*, telling us about its potential; and *feeling*, which evaluates. In summary, feeling is evaluative while emotion/affect is experiential. In part, it is these definitions that mark out the Jungian territory on affect as something distinct from the Freudian approach to this topic. Consequently, it is important to understand the psychoanalytic origins of the notion of affect. While film studies may not have paid much attention to the idea of affect it has been central to psychoanalysis. Chris Hauke puts it succinctly, noting: 'It is impossible to imagine the beginnings of psychoanalysis without the concept of affect. It is as essential a foundation stone as the unconscious mind, the mechanism of repression and the hysterical symptom'.[2]

As hinted at by Hauke, Freud's suggestion was that affect was intimately connected with the mechanisms of repression and the hysterical symptom. His novel approach came about as he hypothesized that repressed emotions needed to be re-experienced and released in a moment of catharsis. He theorized that by once again connecting with these repressed experiences, their effect and power on the analysand would be neutralized. In turn, because the symptoms were the result of the repression, they would subsequently disappear. In this sense, Freud suggested that the symptom was an index of the repressed affect.

> Affects, emotions and their expression in behaviour were a recognised, if still problematic, aspect of humanity, but for psychoanalysis to formulate a theory which explained how these same affects may also become repressed, dammed up and rechannelled into behavioural expression that appeared disconnected from the original affect, was something new. Freud's original method was also novel: it was suggested that, through the manipulation of a cathartic re-experiencing of repressed

emotions, that the symptoms connected with them would cease to have a function and would then disappear...The concept of affect and its repression was, and is now, central to what many think psychoanalysis is all about.[3]

As Freud's thinking developed he became increasingly convinced that the hysterical symptoms that appeared as a consequence of the repression found their origins in sexual material. This led to the formation of the theory of the Oedipal complex supported by the notions of the primal scene, voyeurism and eventually *thanatos* (the death drive or instinct) and *eros* (the drive for life). The suggestion was that the Oedipal situation was a universal part of the human experience and that it had an existence outside time, place, culture or personal upbringing. The absolute impossibility of the situation, and social and cultural taboos, meant that repression was the only tenable course of action. However, as well as presenting itself in the form of hysterical symptoms, the affected force of this repressed material could 'slip out' in a variety of ways, including dreams and inadvertent linguistic *faux pas*. Its sublimation could also manifest itself in all manner of bodily experiences such as eating or excreting its associated disorders. Freud suggested that when the origins of these symptoms and experiences were uncovered they would lose power and normal life could be resumed. Thus, the aetiology of sexual neurosis was well and truly established as a central canonical principle of psychoanalytic theory.

> Freud developed the theory of psychoanalysis in a trajectory that begins with hysterical trauma and the repression of affect, proceeds to a theory of sexuality and the Oedipus complex, and eventually the meta-theorising of the Life and Death instincts. In this Freud displays an effort to reconceive a psychoanalytic science that is less reliant on the rational/emotional split of its beginnings.[4]

In suggesting that the Freudian and Jungian positions may not be so far apart, Hauke's final comment is partly a welcoming gesture towards the Freudian community. Of course, he is right to suggest that both positions probably have more in common than is normally recognized, because, after all, Jung's thinking undeniable grew out of exposure to psychoanalytic ideas. While such bridge-building is appropriate, it remains the case that from the Freudian perspective affect is intimately connected with instincts (or drives) and that it is both repressed and experienced as hysterical symptom. A useful summary is given by Jean Laplanche and J.-B. Pontalis.

> It [affect] connotes any affective state, whether painful or pleasant, whether vague or well defined, and whether it is manifested in a form of a massive discharge or in the form of a general mood. According to Freud, each instinct expresses itself in terms of affect and in terms of ideas (*Vorstellungen*). The affect is the qualitative expression of the quantity of instinctual energy and of its fluctuations.[5]

It is curious that film theory, and psychoanalytic film theory in particular as typified by its existence in the academy, has not incorporated this central notion within its theoretical matrix – perhaps sensing that some of the foundations of the western intellectual tradition are under scrutiny. Disappointingly, the discourse of film theory has yet to find a central a space within which questions of emotion and affect can be articulated. Ayako Saito has noticed this and draws attention to what media studies terms a 'significant absence'. Writing about Hitchcock she notes:

> The purpose of my investigation is to explore the question of affect in film analysis. It seems to me that this question has attracted too little theoretical attention within psychoanalytic film theory. This lack of emphasis may be partly due to the fact that it is considered to belong to the empirical realm. However, I would suggest that the neglect of affect by theory is also largely due to the strong emphasis on the Lacanian psychoanalytic model, which revolves around questions of language and the gaze.[6]

As Saito suggests the dominant modes of psychoanalytic film theory derive partly from structural linguistics, and partly from the Lacanian variant of psychoanalysis which was favoured by the largely theoretical journal *Screen*. Those interests were only partly in film. A central component of the work of *Screen* was political: they deployed whatever analytical tools might prove useful in deconstructing the subject, be they semiotic, structural, genre based or whatever. This said, an emphasis on structuralism and semiotics gave the project a long-standing indebtedness to structural linguistics. The overarching aim of *Screen* was to reveal how ideological messages were inscribed into media texts. As such, psychoanalysis served a useful purpose in revealing how levels of patriarchal construction and repression were hegemonized into films, and to a lesser extent television programmes. To that end, psychoanalysis was not used as a psychoanalytic tool, but as a political weapon.

Given the overtly political nature of their work it is perhaps not too surprising that *Screen* had little time for 'ephemera' such as emotions, (although I am given to understand that meetings of the editorial board where not without their heated debates). Essentially, *Screen* set the agenda for film studies for decades and this partially explains why the current focus of the discipline rests where it does. Its influence was pervasive and interestingly many of the members of *Society for Education in Film and Television*, which owned *Screen* in its most important period, were responsible for the translation and editing of a wide range of criticism which they thought might generally prove useful to their ends. Amongst this was the work of cinema theorist Christian Metz.

While Metz started with an interest in cinema, semiotics and language, he later came to include psychoanalysis within his analytic pantheon. Like *Screen*, Metz was not much interested in emotions, but in *Psychoanalysis and Cinema* he had the following observation to make:

> The adult spectator, who belongs to a social group that watches films seated and silent – he, in short (that other sort of native), who is neither a child nor childlike – finds himself without defences, if the film touches him profoundly or if he is in a state of fatigue or emotional turmoil, etc., against those brief moments of mental seesawing which each of us has experienced and which bring him a step closer to true illusion. This approach to a strong (or stronger) type of belief in the diegesis is a

bit like the brief and quickly passing dizziness that drivers feel towards the end of a long night journey (of which film is one).[7]

Yet even here the concern is with how film might activate feelings if the viewer's defences are down. The diegesis that Metz refers to is composed of the techniques of classic realist cinema – the rules of continuity editing – by which a film appears to be a single unfolding seamless narrative. Interestingly, there is no sense from Metz that an emotional response might be appropriate or necessary. There is certainly no sense that feelings can be as discriminatory and evaluative as thinking.

As already mentioned, Jungian psychology, by blending the terms 'emotion' and 'affect', and with its differentiation of 'feeling' as an *evaluative* response, has the capacity to redress this imbalance. Therefore, even though feelings are one of the expressions of emotions, for our purposes the evaluative nature of feeling needs to be kept separate from the experience of affect. The editors of the *Critical Dictionary of Jungian Analysis* put it like this:

> [Affect] Synonymous with emotion; feeling of sufficient intensity to cause nervous agitation or other obvious psychomotor disturbances. One has command over feeling, whereas affect intrudes against one's will and can only be repressed with difficulty. An explosion of affect is an invasion of the individual and a temporary takeover of the ego.[8]

The important point about this is that the experience of affect points towards something that is meaningful or true about ourselves, or about our current life situation. The suggestion is that affect is in essence a communication from the objective psyche and, as established, the motivations of the psyche are towards growth, awareness and integration. This tendency of the psyche towards health is encapsulated in the Jungian cornerstone of an unconscious that is teleological and positive. Thus, it is vital that attention is paid to emotion, or affect. James Hillman puts it like this:

> Emotion always has some survival value and reveals some truth about reality, but this truth is symbolic, not merely sociological or biological. We cannot therefore condemn an emotion without giving it full hearing, without trying to grasp the transformation as symbolic. In short, emotion, no matter how bizarre, must be taken in awful earnest before diagnosing it abortive.[9]

Put another way, affect has as important role to play in the psyche as rationality.

For Jung, the archetype is especially known by its affectual tone which accompanies the imagery, cognition and behaviour manifested by archetypal activity. Emotions are the way human beings know themselves and the world and in this respect are equal to the role played by rational thought. In Jung's view of the psyche, affect seems to become the subjectively experienced equivalent of what is otherwise described by the abstract terms of psychic energy or libido.[10]

Later it will be seen that the act of viewing films involves an affective, emotional response that is akin to the experience of the ego when it is being affected by the unconscious. As such it is central to the cinematic experience.

While Jungian and Freudian psychology may have a different understanding of what constitutes affect they both agree that it is a central and core component of the psyche. This is not surprising as in formulating his theoretical position on the role of affect, Jung had been influenced by Eugen Bleuler's work. Jung joined Bleuler at the Berghölzli hospital in 1903 and continued to work there until 1909 when he left to set up his personal practice at Küsnacht. (The reasons for the move appear to have been a combination of work-load and theoretical differences.) Midway through his time at Berghölzli (in 1906) he published a review of Bleuler's *Affektivität, Suggestibilität, Paranoia* in which he commented:

> Affectivity is of the greatest imaginable importance in psychopathology. Quite apart from the affective psychoses proper (manic-depressive insanity), it plays a significant role in psychoses which one was wont to regard as predominantly intellectual... He [Bleuler] found that the content of the paranoid picture developed from a *feeling-toned complex*, that is, from ideas accompanied by intensive affect which therefore have an abnormally strong influence on the psyche.[11]

The crucial point here is that Jung established a link between affect and the *feeling-toned* complex. In analytical psychology the complex is made up of a series of images, ideas and responses that have a quasi-autonomous existence within the psyche. As such the complex can be thought of as a sub, or splinter, personality.

> The complex was seen as deriving its particular significance as a vortex of emotional energy from the functioning of archetypal activity in the psyche. *This perspective places affect or emotion centrally within the dynamics of the psyche and not in contrast or opposition to so-called 'rationality'.*[12]

There are numerous illustrations of this formulation in Jung's writing, but he gives a particularly clear statement of the relationship between complex and affect in the following example from 1923:

> A very naughty child who has caused his mother a lot of trouble might say: 'I didn't mean to, I didn't want hurt you, I love you too much'. Such explanations appeal to the existence of a different kind of personality from the one that appeared in the affect. In both cases the affective personality appears as something inferior that seized hold of the real ego and obscured it. But often the personality revealed in the affect is a higher and better one, so much so that, regrettably, one cannot remain on such a pinnacle of perfection. We all know those sudden fits of generosity, altruism, self-sacrifice, and similar 'beautiful gestures'...[13]

Note here how affect is not just an experience of negative emotions, it can also provide a sense of ego-inflation in which our sense of self-worth and importance is exaggerated.

This may help in understanding the sense of euphoria with which can follow after watching film. The identification with some on-screen heroic or altruistic activity temporarily invades ego-consciousness and for a brief time we are buoyed up by the sense of euphoria which it has released within us.

It is also important to be careful here as the description of the complex as feeling-toned can be misleading. It seems as though Jung is positioning the complex on the feeling-thinking evaluative axis. What is actually being suggested is that the psychic elements clustered around and forming the complex have a common emotional resonance or theme – there is an emotional synergy between each of the parts. As such the complex might also be described as possessing a common *emotional-tone*, but the literature normally uses Jung's original formulation. It is interesting that in 1906, while working with Bleuler, Jung offered a definition of affectivity which certainly encompasses emotion but which also went much further.

> *Affectivity*, comprising all affects and quasi affective processes, is an inclusive concept which covers all non-intellectual psychic processes such as volition, feeling, suggestibility, attention etc. It is a psychic factor that exerts as much influence on the psyche as on the body.[14]

By 1921 Jung was working towards a view of affect that was different to that of Bleuler (who was at the time his senior) in which both the emotional and physiological elements of affect were clearly identified.

> By the term affect I mean a state of feeling characterised by marked physical innervation on the one hand and a peculiar disturbance of the ideational process on the other. I use *emotion* as synonymous with affect. I distinguish – in contrast to Bleuler (v. *Affectivity*)-*feeling* (q.v.) from affect, in spite of the fact that the dividing line is fluid, since every feeling, after attaining a certain strength, releases physical interventions, thus becoming an affect. For practical reasons, however, it is advisable to distinguish affect from feeling, since feeling can be a voluntary disposable function, whereas affect is usually not....I regard affect on the one hand as a psychic feeling-state and on the other as a physiological innervation-state, each of which has a cumulative, reciprocal effect on the other. That is to say, a component of sensation allies itself with the intensified feeling, so that affect is approximated more to *sensation* (q.v.) and essentially differentiated, from the feeling-state.[15]

Published in the same year as this quote, Jung elaborates this position in an article titled *Schiller's Ideas on the Type Problem*. It is striking that his description of object, libido and identification seems to resonate strongly with the experience of viewing films. While reading the quote, note how the libido investment he describes is akin to the process of psychological projection in which part of the viewer's psyche finds an unconscious identification with the on-screen characters. What I want to suggest is that this process is enabled through the mechanism of introjection and that this releases affects that are concomitant with the individual's psychological situation and history. Jung suggests that this then opens up the possibility of psychological transformation. To extrapolate, perhaps the affective power of the cinema has the potential to transform, for the better, the psyche of viewers.

> For, while I am striving to subordinate the object to my will, my whole being is gradually brought into relationship with it, following the strong libido investment which, as it were, draws a portion of my being across into the object. The result of this is a partial identification of certain portions of my personality with similar qualities in the object. As soon as this identification has taken place, the conflict is transferred into my own psyche. This 'introjection' of the conflict with the object creates an inner discord, making me powerless against the object and also releasing affects, which are always symptomatic of inner disharmony. The affects, however, prove that I am sensing myself and am therefore in a position – if I am not blind – to apply my attention to myself and to follow up the play of opposites in my own psyche.[16]

This raises an interesting issue, namely to what extent can the emotional affective state that is awoken by the on-screen fictional worlds of cinema be considered real? In other words, is the affective state a genuine emotional experience or is it in some way a delusion – has ego-consciousness been tricked into taking something illusory as something real? Recently, Jungian orientated film theory has begun to address this issue, but it has to be kept in mind that it is hardly a hot topic and comes someway down the list of concerns after archetype, myth, complex and so on. However, John Izod has made some headway in this matter. In his book, *Myth, Mind and the Screen*, Izod postulates that films, and indeed other fictions, can produce an affective response in their viewers/readers and that this is positive and real, even though the on-screen imagery is clearly not real. (This is an interesting take on the media effects debate, where the power of films and television to influence behaviour is persistently presented in terms of the corrupting power of the media.)

> However, the effects upon audiences of emotions aroused by drama and fictions (including those played out on screen) are in general benign precisely because they refer to a virtual rather than a real world. Story worlds allow for play with emotions just as much as with characters, situations and ideas vicariously experienced. Spectators make discoveries about a hypothetical, not a real, situation.[17]

Izod's suggestion (that benign emotional effects are a result of vicarious play in a virtual world) is an interesting one. It certainly is the case that in Jungian analysis there are numerous techniques which encourage the analysand to enter into a fictional world to therapeutic ends including active imagination, painting, sandplay and dream analysis. Significantly what all these activities have in common is that the fictional world is produced by the analysand. These activities help to break down the defences of consciousness and allow the objective psyche to express in symbolic and visual terms what is going on in the psyche. The resulting images are then worked on within the analytic setting. This is rather different to the viewers' relationship to the on-screen world that has ostensibly been provided for their entertainment. However, this need not be a stumbling block, and Izod suggests that the story world is a virtual world (hence, its benign nature). But if, instead, we adopt the analytic premise that the image is taken as real (that the experience someone has is accepted as real and entered into), we can see more clearly how it is that spectators may make real discoveries about actual aspects of their lives. The benign nature of the fictional world is now due not to its virtual nature but the teleological and positive guiding nature of the objective psyche. This observation lends further support to the point that Izod goes on to make, namely that a viewer's understanding of film can be influenced by his or her unconscious.

> When the action on the screen greatly excites spectators, it seems probable that their emotions set in train the affective process which alters the configuration in the memory of the images even as they are being screened. So the filter through which the unconscious alters and dissolves images and narrative events in conformity with its own predispositions may be assumed to begin its action at once.[18]

This psychological approach to a structuralist observation is well made and links nicely with Izod's suggestion that the work of interpreting a film happens after the film has been seen. On the face of it this would seem a reasonable claim, as clearly it is not possible to understand a film before we have watched it.

> Spectators are likely, therefore, to allow themselves a form of play in which for the moment they adopt, without the risk of becoming locked into it, one of the virtual roles that, as a transitional phenomenon, the film has prepared for them...But after the film has ended, active imagination takes over and develops the recollected cinematic imagery by fusing it more completely with personal fantasy material. In the process both are liable to change.[19]

Again this seems to be along the right lines but does not quite go far enough. Film theory certainly suggests that within each movie there is a central identification figure. However, the viewer may or may not identify with that figure, or may instead choose a more marginal character in the film. This said, the film is created with the assumption that most viewers will focus on the central character. One way of reading, or interpreting, the narrative space of the film is as an expression of the inner state of the central identification figure. His or her inner psychological concerns and attitudes take on a visual form within the film – story space becomes psychological space, if you will. But it is also the case that during the act of watching a film that personal psychological material can be activated. In line with Izod's point above viewers bring their own concerns *as* they experience a film, not *just* afterwards. What happens is that when watching films a transformative space is created; the film becomes part transitional object (that seems like me, that is not like me) and is also a place where affect invades ego-consciousness with potentially transformative consequences. Here, it is important to bear in mind the primacy of the objective psyche and the reality of the affect it can activate. Nagy points us in the right direction:

> ...[the] powerful affective states which Jungians call archetypal are frequently accompanied by spontaneous images which may appear in dreams, semi-conscious fantasies, or may even be projectively vested in outer objects...Affectivity is of the very stuff of Jung's view of archetypes. It is for him the substance of the real.[20]

Jung is also quite clear on this point. He distinguishes between the psyche in its affective and 'authentic' states but notes that in both conditions the ego remains the same. This is consummate with the core Jungian principle that any experience of the psyche must be treated as psychologically real. Importantly, he also notes that because the affective state overwhelms consciousness it is seen as unproblematic, while by contrast the normal state of affairs requires us to discriminate, make decisions and take responsibility for our actions.

> Since it is impossible to deny the pertinence of the affective state to the ego, it follows that the ego is the same ego whether in the affective state or in the so-called 'authentic' state, even though it displays a differential attitude to these psychological happenings. In the affective state it is unfree, driven, coerced. By contract, the normal state is a state of free will, with all one's powers at one's disposal. In other words *the affective state is unproblematical, while the normal state is problematical: it comprises both the problem and possibility of free choice.* In this latter state an understanding becomes possible, because in it alone can one discern one's motives and gain self-knowledge.[21]

What Jung is driving at is that from the subjective point of view the affective state *seems* unproblematic. The person experiencing the affect does not see the problem because they are immersed in it. Again, there is a remarkable degree of correspondence between this description and the state of the viewer while watching a film. For example, while watching the on-screen world it seems unproblematic to the viewer, even though it has the capacity to awaken emotions that would in other contexts be quite disturbing. Even though these emotions can be intense, the collective nature of the experience exerts its presence and holds the audience in its seats as different emotions and psycho-physical affective responses play themselves out in the film's spectators. The driven nature of the affect released by the cinematic mechanisms of the on-screen world also serves to keep the audience where it is. After all, as spectators we know that this experience will be relatively short, we know (unlike experiences of affect in the real world) that watching a film will be a relatively short experience and that our normal state of being will shortly be restored. However, as Jung notes the work of transformation occurs after the affective state, as it is only at this point that the psyche can discriminate and gain 'self-knowledge'. It is, therefore, the case that cinema screened films contain both affective-emotional elements and allow for the possibility of the feeling-toned evaluative response to their contents. As we come to understand why certain films move us, overtake us, and overwhelm us, the psyche becomes increasingly differentiated – the movies have the capacity to help us understand more fully who we are.

In summary, the suggestion is that cinema screened films awaken in their spectators an emotional-affective state – it is a state that also has the capacity to awaken within us an evaluative response, not to the film itself, but to our reactions to it. During the actual viewing of the film, this is something that is achieved through the mechanisms of Hollywood 'realist' film-making by which a believable on-screen diegetic world is established and the processes of projection and identification are enabled. In the language of film theory, the viewer is stitched, or *sutured*, into the world of the film and the gulf between viewer and screen in temporarily breached. Each viewer may have a quite individual affective response to a film as personal complexes are activated, projected onto the screen and subsequently introjected into the psyche. The temporary nature of this viewing experience lets spectators experience intense emotions that would normally be disturbing. After watching a film the psyche returns to its normal state, which gives the opportunity for reflection and insight into the responses that have been awoken. One of the psychological functions of the cinematic experience is to offer us the potential to know ourselves more and to come to a fuller understanding of who we are.

Notes

1. Schiller, H. *Information Inequality: The Deepening Social Crisis in America*. (London: Routledge, 1996), p. 65.
2. Hauke, C. *Jung and the Postmodern: The Interpretation of Realities*. (London: Routledge, 2000), p. 227.
3. *Ibid.*, p. 227–8.
4. *Ibid.*, p. 230.
5. Laplanche, L. and Pontalis, J. B. *The Language of Psychoanalysis*. (London: Karnak Books, 1988), p. 13, cited in Saito, A. *Hitchcock's Trilogy: A Logic of Mise-en-Scène*. In Bergstrom, J. (ed.), *Endless Night: Cinema and Psychoanalysis, Parallel Histories*. (Berkeley: University of California Press, 1999), p. 202.
6. Saito, A. *Hitchcock's Trilogy: A Logic of Mise-en-Scène*. In Bergstrom, J. (ed.), *Endless Night: Cinema and Psychoanalysis, Parallel Histories*. Berkeley: University of California Press, 1999, p. 201.
7. Metz, C. *Psychoanalysis and Cinema: The Imaginary Signifier*. Trans., Guzzetti *et al.* (London: Macmillan Press, 1982), p. 103.
8. Samuels, A., Shorter, B., and Plaut, F., (eds) *A Critical Dictionary of Jungian Analysis*. (London: Routledge and Kegan Paul, 1986), p. 11.
9. Hillman, J. *Emotion: A Comprehensive Phenomenology of Theories and Their Meanings for Therapy*. (London: Routledge and Kegan Paul, 1960), pp. 282–3.
10. Hauke, C. *Jung and the Postmodern: The Interpretation of Realities*. (London: Routledge, 2000), p. 231–2.
11. Jung, C. G. (1976) *Collected Works* vol. 18. London: Routledge and Kegan Paul, para. 889. Emphasis as original.
12. Hauke, C. *Jung and the Postmodern: The Interpretation of Realities*. (London: Routledge, 2000), p. 231. Emphasis as original.
13. Jung, C. G. (1964/71) *Collected Works* vol. 6. (London: Routledge and Kegan Paul), para. 889–890.
14. Jung, C. G. (1976) *Collected Works* vol. 18. (London: Routledge and Kegan Paul), para. 888. Emphasis as original.
15. Jung, C. G. (1964/71) *Collected Works* vol. 6. London: Routledge and Kegan Paul, para. 681. Emphasis as original.
16. *Ibid.*, para. 137.
17. Izod, J. *Myth, Mind and the Screen: Understanding the Heroes of Our Time*. (Cambridge: Cambridge University Press, 2001), pp. 15–16.

18. *Ibid.*, p. 17.
19. *Ibid.*, p. 17.
20. Nagy, M. *Philosophical Issues in the Psychology of C. G. Jung.* (Albany: State University of New York Press, 1991), p. 111.
21. Jung, C. G. (1964/71) *Collected Works* vol. 6. (London: Routledge and Kegan Paul), para. 891. Emphasis as original.

3

Chinatown: Investigating Affect

Chinatown – A Plot Synopsis

Hollis Mulwray (Darrell Zwerling) is the chief engineer of the water and power department. Ida Sessions (Diane Ladd) pretends to be his wife, Evelyn Cross Mulwray, and asks Private Investigator Jake Gittes (Jack Nicholson) to investigate what she believes to be her husband's adulterous activities. In a separate strand to the narrative, Hollis is actively opposing a plan to build a dam which would provide drinking water for Los Angeles. As part of his investigation, Gittes observes Hollis examining a dry riverbed and he also photographs Hollis with a young woman, and Jakes assumes Hollis is having an affair with her. Once the story hits the press, the real Mrs Mulwray appears in Gittes' office threatening to sue if he doesn't drop the case immediately.

In a surprising turn of events Hollis is found drowned in a run-off water channel and Jake decides to investigate. Ida Sessions (who impersonated Evelyn Mulwray) advises him to read the obituary column in the newspaper. Evelyn continues with her story that her husband was having an affair. Gittes tells her that her husband was murdered and that he believes she is still hiding something. Evelyn Mulwray hires Gittes to find out how her husband died.

Gittes discovers a plot to buy cheap, unwatered land for low prices, to irrigate it and then sell it at a profit. He visits an orange grove where he learns that the city Water Board has been poisoning the water. He explains to Evelyn that farmers are being driven off their land and that it is being purchased in the name of elderly and recently deceased people to protect the identity of the real purchasers. He tells her that Hollis knew of this plan and that was why he was murdered. Eventually, Gittes has an affair with Evelyn. It clear that she is anxious that he has been talking to her father, who she suggests might be 'behind all this'. Evelyn drives to the house and Gittes follows her. The mysterious girl who Gittes thought Hollis was having an affair with is there – it transpires that she is Evelyn's sister.

Back at his home Gittes gets a phone call telling him to meet with Ida Sessions but on arriving he discovers she has been murdered. The police at the crime scene tell Gittes that Hollis Mulwray drowned in salt water. He goes back to the Mulwray's to find that Evelyn is getting ready to leave. He goes back to the house where Evelyn and her sister are getting ready to leave for Mexico. Evelyn confirms that the glasses are her husband's and reveals the terrible truth that the girl (Katherine) is both her sister and her daughter. Gittes asks if her father raped her – she shakes her head.

Gittes arranges for his associates to meet him in *Chinatown*. He telephones Cross saying that he has the girl at his daughter's house. On arriving Gittes confronts Cross about killing Hollis Mulwray. At gunpoint Gittes leads them to the meeting place in *Chinatown*. Jake is arrested and handcuffed, along with his associates. Evelyn shoots her father but the police return fire, killing Evelyn. Katherine is left alive but distraught.

The purpose of this chapter is not so much to provide an example of how an affect-informed film analysis works but rather it shows how a range of Jungian concepts and techniques can be useful when analysing films. This said, it is inevitable that notions of affect will crop up particularly when reflecting on those points in Roman Polanski's *Chinatown* (1974) that seem particularly illogical or strange. A consideration of affect is also central in understanding the final sequences in the film – the traumatic moment of narrative disclosure which provides the film's most distressing moments.

This broad Jungian interpretation of the film offers a different perspective to that provided by more established theoretical frameworks. The suggestion is that by looking at the symbolic structure of the film it is possible to offer an alternative and yet coherent reading that makes sense of some of the film's apparently strange and somewhat disjointed imagery. This also goes someway into explaining the strange mixture of feelings that the film can evoke in viewers. Some find it boring while by contrast others find it too disturbing to watch. I have watched this film repeatedly over the last twenty years or so and, without really knowing why, it has fascinated me. As a result of working on this analysis it has been possible to get a little closer to understanding the range of conflicting emotions that the film can awaken and so become aware of the emotional discord which chimes throughout the narrative.

Perhaps *Chinatown* would not be everyone's first choice as a movie to examine from a psychological perspective. It does not fall in the quasi-canonical films beloved of film theorists with a psychoanalytic background; films with more obviously redolent psychological imagery tend to be their preferred hunting ground. Somewhat discouragingly, it is also the case that much of the critical work carried out on *Chinatown* tends to adopt broadly political and economic modes of analysis. Typical of this approach is Michael Eaton's useful interpretation of the film. In his book Eaton examines the form of the film and carefully locates it both historically and technologically. In looking at content he places the film within the broader body of Polanski's work and also at a specific moment in film history. A distinctive section of the book explores the relationship between Vladimir Propp's structural analysis of literary narrative in *Morphology of the Folktale* before introducing an account of rites of passage as derived from the work of Arnold an Gennep. These sections follow a brief allusion to Joseph Campbell's monomyth of the hero's journey. Even though Eaton is close to what might traditionally be thought of as Jungian territory, his analysis of the film remains more classical than psychological as its focus is on the aesthetic and formal elements of *Chinatown*. On this note, it is striking that the central theme of the film, which serves to drive the film's narrative (albeit, under the surface of the film for much of the time), namely the issue of incest, is dealt with in a couple of paragraphs (pp. 61–62).

There is the distinct possibility that the analysis in the forthcoming pages goes too far in the opposite direction in giving the more surreal, mythological and psychological elements of the narrative an undue prominence. This said, the intention is to take a film which is well known and to attempt to re-frame it. In so doing certain aspects of the narrative and its visual/symbolic structure come to the foreground. Do they obscure the more materialist elements of the film? Perhaps so, but the hope is that these elements of the film are familiar enough for the psychological observations to sit alongside them. It is also true that this analysis is firmly based in the material basis of the film's cinematic imagery. The argument here is not one of interpretative superiority, rather it is one of synergy and complementarity. The psychological view of the film does not supersede other interpretations, it is not necessarily better or more comprehensive but what it does offer is a view which has been marginalized within mainstream film theory.

It might seem perverse to tackle a film which most commentators agree is not particularly psychological from a post-Jungian perspective. Yet there is also merit in considering a film that is not explicitly psychological from a psychological vantage point. Why would this be so? One reason is that films which set out to explore psychological themes are often overly rationalized and, perhaps, sanitized. The self-conscious structure of Nicholas Roeg's films, for example, certainly provides fertile ground for psychoanalytic film theorists. Yet the films are also too knowing, too aware of their intentions for the unconscious to run wild. Films that intentionally set out to explore psychological themes might end up with a product which is actually less psychologically interesting than a more apparently mundane piece of popular culture.

While writing about literature, the observations that Jung made in his article from 1930 seem to hold good for cinema too. Jung is arguing for non-psychological material to be taken seriously. This stems directly from his experiences in the consulting room where clients may introduce material that they do not realize has psychological significance. In such a case it is the role of the analyst to be alert to these developments and to work with the client in helping them to understand the value of what they have brought. So too aspects of popular culture may not self-consciously set out to explore psychological themes but the film analyst is in a strong position to spot such unwitting psychological ramifications. As Jung notes:

> In general, it is the non-psychological novel that offers the richest opportunities for psychological elucidation. Here the author, having no intentions of this sort, does not show his characters in a psychological light and thus leaves room for analysis and

interpretation, or even invites it by his unprejudiced mode of presentation. Good examples of such novels are those of Benoît, or English fiction after the manner of Rider Haggard, as well as the most popular article of literary mass-production, the detective story, first exploited by Conan Doyle.[1]

At one level *Chinatown* is clearly a knowing film. Its characters are tightly drawn, its intertextual references to other *film noir* movies are intentional and clear, as are the allusions it makes to previous films by Polanski. It is both generically and authorially strong. This said, there are points at which the film seems more intuitive, such moments being somewhat out of place in a film which ostensibly deals with the murky world of big business, corporate corruption and city politics. For example, a boy sitting on a horse in a dried up riverbed, sheep bursting into a council hearing and the image of the albacore (a tuna), which runs throughout the film, all seem curiously at odds with the film's central themes. The characters in the film are odd too and are largely without life. While Noah Cross (John Huston) acts in a thoroughly reprehensible manner, it is hard to have strong feelings towards him. Little is known about Jack Gittes (Jack Nicholson), except that he fits the bill of the typical *film noir* private investigator – a loner, with a wry take on life who trusts his instincts every bit as much as his intellect. Evelyn Mulwray (Faye Dunaway) is emotionally remote, troubled and anxious, worried that one day the dreadful truth about her life will eventually be exposed and she as more than a hint of the *femme fatale* about her. In short, the film is seemingly populated more by stock characters than fully developed individuals.

Despite these apparent shortcomings the film remains intriguing. This is partly due to its fairly slow-burning narrative which finally erupts in the closing moments of the film. This outburst of affect occurs as the audience becomes aware of the extent to which unconscious fantasies have been acted on. Admittedly, there are plenty of other less compelling moments but there is a hook in this film that keeps viewers coming back. It also regularly keeps *Chinatown* high in the numerous lists of top 100 movies. (At the time of writing its current ranking by the Internet Movie Database is forty-second – http://www.imdb.com/chart/top). This raises the prospect that the film is compelling not just because its narrative is interesting but because it also communicates at the levels of affect, symbol and the unconscious. Underneath the visual surface of the film there is a concealed symbolic structure which Jungian psychology can help to reveal, although, to be fair, this psychological appeal belongs to the detective genre as much as the film.

Interestingly, Jung drew a parallel between detective stories and cinema. In so doing he makes a more general point about the way that fictional narratives can give expression to cultural symptoms and, in so doing, also meet a need for vicarious experience.

The cinema, like the detective story, enables us to experience without danger to ourselves all the excitements, passions and fantasies which have o be repressed in a humanistic age. It is not difficult to see how these symptoms link up with our psychological situation.[2]

In the article Jung is concerned with the need for humankind to accept that the split between body and spirit is an artificial one. His view is that the one gives expression to the other. If the term 'spirit' is off-putting then instead consider the possibility that we possess an unconscious and that this part of ourselves, of which we are not yet fully aware, exists in relationship to our body. One of the roles of analytical psychotherapy is to facilitate an individual's reflection on the totality of their lived experience. In so doing, the intention is to make explicit what had been implicit (or put another way, to make conscious what had been unconscious). In the preceding quote, Jung suggests that the detective might have a similar role.

Curiously, the arrival of the detective as an individual investigator originates in the middle part of the nineteenth century, at around the same time as the birth of psychoanalysis. The figure was the product of popular culture (rather than high literature) and, by and large, remains so today. It is, therefore, not surprising that the detective lives and works in the city. He is at home in its labyrinthine streets and while he is part of the city he also remains somewhat outside it. As a loner he lacks both the ability, and need, for intimate relationships. While he is not immune to the allure of a *femme fatale*, he is also afraid of what he perceives to be her destructive qualities. But as a man on the quest for truth, law and order, he will do whatever is necessary to solve a crime. No matter what the city, the American detective has an affinity with its *Chinatown*. This is both part of the greater metropolis but it is also different – it is a place of otherness. The detective, then, is a transgressive character, going where he should not in order to seek out the truth.

A traditional Freudian psychoanalytic interpretation of the detective story seeks to unearth the psychoanalytic secret on which the narrative is predicated. It turns out that the secret is always the same, the crime being the child's murderous desire to kill the parent of the opposite sex and to have the remaining parent to themselves. The standard detective narrative then seeks to mobilize the viewer's unconscious Oedipal desires and to have them played out on the screen. The detective takes on the role of the child in gradually trying to piece together exactly what is going on in the parent's bedroom. According to the theory, whether the reaction to the primal scene of the child viewing the parent's having sex has been denial or acceptance, the repressed memory remains charged with affect. The detective story attempts to present a more satisfying, less painful, if fictional, primal scene. In an orgy of investigation the child as the ego is personified in the figure of the detective. The child witnessing the primal scene fears castration as a punishment for his Oedipal desires and this prohibition ensures the desires are not acted on. Unlike the child the detective as an adult experiences no such anxiety and, for that reason, is able to provide an altogether less traumatic version of the family romance.

However, in the case of *Chinatown* there is a literal acting out of the Oedipal fantasy. Evelyn and Noah, as father and daughter, have a daughter themselves, Katherine (Belinda Palmer). As might be expected the detective (Jack Gittes) stand as the child/ego – the sibling enquiring into the mysteries of the family romance. He is duly punished for his inquisitiveness by having his nose cut (symbolic castration), a violent act that is carried by an unnamed character played by Polanski himself. Is it too much to suggest that the director of the film is punishing the audience as represented by Gittes for their interest in such murky material? That Gittes has an affair with Evelyn, who in a sense is symbolically mother and child, only serves to reinforce the incestuous root of the film.

However, there are other psychological ways to read this film. While the narrative undoubtedly does have these Freudian concerns, it also deals with the theme of incest from quite a different perspective. However, to get to this point it is necessary to explore some of its other less immediate concerns. This will eventually lead to a re-examination of the centrality of the incest motif in *Chinatown*. In *Chinatown* nothing and no one are quite what they first seem to be. Hollis Mulwray (Darrell Zwerling) appears to be having an affair, yet he turns out to be the most faithful of husbands, protecting, as he does, Evelyn's secret and her child. A retirement home provides the clue which helps Gittes get to the root of corrupt business practices. Noah Cross, ostensibly an astute business man, turns out to be corrupt both in the political and moral sense.

Further, from the opening moments of the film the audience find themselves in a world that is familiar but also strange. The opening titles are instantly recognizable as those of Paramount Pictures, but here the studio's trademark logo of the mountain with its overarching stars has been presented in the form of a sepia tint.[3] An ethereal sounding glissando is followed by the main theme of the movie on a solo trumpet. These musical motifs reoccur throughout the film at key points. The glissando acting as a *leitmotif* suggesting that something unworldly or uncanny is unfolding. The overall effect of these different elements is to defamiliarize the familiar and to subtly unsettle the audience. In its opening, *Chinatown* evokes nostalgia for a time that never was, for a childhood that should have been perfect but which in reality was painful. The image belongs to the culture as much as to the narrative of the film – this is a story which is entering a world which longs to find a child-like innocence but which actually compels viewers to come face-to-face with their inner anxieties.

Opening Titles *Chinatown*

It is only in retrospect, and probably for most audiences on repeated viewings of *Chinatown*, that it is possible to recognize the significance of the film's opening sequence, J. J. Gittes' office. Jack is breaking the bad news to Curly (Burt Young) that his wife has been unfaithful. To Curly's evident distress, Gittes presents the photographic evidence. By trade, Curly is a tuna fisherman, and the albacore tuna is integral to *Chinatown*'s story, and so from the start the audience is presented with unlikely association of adultery to the seemingly unconnected image of water. Curly does not make another appearance until the end of the film when he has a key role to play in Gittes' plan to save Evelyn and her daughter. In a similar vein the audience are wrong-footed on their first encounter with Evelyn Mulwray. In the opening minutes of the film Evelyn arrives at Gittes' office. Like Curly, suspects that her spouse is having an affair and wants the matter investigated. Gittes advises her to leave the matter alone but is eventually persuaded to take up the case. He soon discovers that his services have been engaged by an impostor; the real Mrs Mulwray preferring matters to be left firmly alone.

This opening lays out the film's themes. By way of a familiar greeting, the Paramount Pictures logo invites the audience into the film while at the same time it warns that this is not going to be a comfortable couple of hours. A fisherman, a worker and cuckold becomes a figure the detective is going to depend on. So too the audience is asked to trust Gittes, although he is self-evidently an untrustworthy and shifty character. Illusion as a theme in this film has a distinctly psychological and unconscious quality. Jung provides a reminder that the unconscious operates along different lines to those of the rational world. For him one of the guiding principles of the psyche is that it is structured around what may appear to be opposites but which in fact turn out to exist in a compensatory and balancing relationship. To reprise a quote from chapter one:

> But what is 'illusion'? By what criterion do we judge something to be an illusion? Does anything exist for the psyche that we are entitled to call illusion? Presumably the psyche does not trouble itself about our categories of reality; for it, everything that *works* is real...[4]

Later in the same paragraph Jung comments, 'To takes these realities for what they are – not foisting other names on them – that is our businesses. To the psyche, spirit is no less spirit for being named sexuality'.[5] It is sexual desire that is at the heart of *Chinatown*. But as with much else in the film, suggestions of sex are not what they appear. Far from having an affair, Hollis Mulwray turns out to be looking after his wife's child. Somehow the images of fatherhood, sex and masculinity sit uncomfortably alongside each other.

Chinatown, as a location, actually hardly features at all in the film. Instead, it stands as a sort of metaphor, against which the narrative is set. In a way, the film's *Chinatown* is reminiscent of the deep archetypal structures in the psyche; while they are invisible, their effects are nonetheless felt. So too *Chinatown*'s only significant appearance as a location is in the final minutes of the film, but it is referred to regularly in the dialogue.

In the following conversation the contradictory nature of *Chinatown* seems to spill out from the confines of the city to affect Evelyn and Gittes' relationship.

Evelyn   Why does it bother you to talk about the past?

Gittes   It bothers everybody who works there. *Chinatown*, everybody. To me it was just bad luck.

Evelyn   Why?

Gittes   You can't always tell what's going on. Like with you.

Eveyln   Why was it bad luck?

Gittes   I was trying to keep someone from being hurt. I ended up making sure she was hurt.

This theme, of matters not being as they appear to be, is continued in the film's use of photographic imagery. In keeping with what might be thought of as the *enantiodromaic* (the running together of what seemly are opposites) nature of the film, photographs both reveal and obscure narrative details. The photographs which open the film revealed to Curly the reality that his wife was having an affair. The photographs taken in Echo Park of Hollis and Katherine misdirect the audience into wrongly confirming Gittes' suspicion that Hollis too is an adulterer. The same is true of their photographs taken by Gittes from a rooftop. The image shown on screen of the camera lens has Hollis and Katherine the 'right' way up. Which, of course, is the wrong way around as in reality their reflection would in reality have been inverted on the camera lens. During the director's commentary of the DVD there is some discussion of this moment, and Polanski remarks that he would re-invert the image if he were to re-shoot the scene. However, the image as it stands in the film has a subtly unsettling effect. Mirroring many of the relationships in the film, the audience is left with the sense that something is wrong, even if it is not clear exactly what that might be. (Perhaps this is an example of where the original intuition of the director is best left alone and not interfered with by subsequent, conscious, reflection.)

Jack Nicholson (Jake Gittes) on surveillance *Chinatown*

Jack's story hits the newspapers *Chinatown*

Next come the front pages of the newspapers which again serve to perpetuate the myth that Hollis is having an affair while at the same time revealing Jack Gittes' love of publicity. Two further photographs serve to point the viewer towards what is actually happening in the film. The first of these is the image of Evelyn with a horse and is accompanied by a reprise of the glissando. Again the effect is to create a somewhat unsettling, almost eerie atmosphere. Finally, the photograph of Noah Cross at the offices of the Water Board suggests to both Gittes and the audience that Evelyn is in some way linked to Noah Cross. It is only later it is revealed she is his daughter.

One of the interpretative tools used in Jungian analysis to uncover the psychological meaning of images is the process of amplification. This involves the analyst in the work of finding parallels for a given image in other myths. The intention is to erode our conscious defences and to work intuitively in finding links, associations and eventually meanings. This approach is not without its difficulties. After all, there is no logical reason to assume that just because a similar image appears in another narrative, perhaps hundreds of years earlier and from another culture, that it will have any relevance. Yet this is precisely what Jungian amplification suggests. The theoretical reasons for this are not entirely clear. Some argue that as the structure of the psyche is relatively constant across culture and time so too its imagery takes on a semi-predictable quality. However, another possibility is that it is the analyst's own unconscious projections that become mobilized. What the analyst is then faced with is material that might be the client's or which might be the analyst's. There is nothing new in this suggestion as it is, after all, the basis upon which transference and counter-transference is predicated. It is also not unreasonable to suggest that while any act of interpretation is partly based on the evidence presented by the narrative it is also the result of perceptive insights by the interpreter.

With this *caveat* in mind it is certainly possible to see a fairly consistent pattern in the imagery of the film and one that can reasonably be regarded as having something of a mythological quality. Finding a correspondence between Noah Cross (who, along with

Hollis Wulwray, owned the Water Department) and the biblical Noah does not require a great leap of intuition. Where it gets more interesting is that unlike his biblical namesake, Noah Cross has a dark sinister side. The lunchtime meeting of Jack Gittes and Noah Cross occurs almost exactly at the mid-point of the film; it also provides the first mention of *Chinatown* where he describes his relationship with Lou Escobar (Perry Lopez),

Gittes   We used to work together, in *Chinatown*.
Cross   Would you call him a capable man?
Gittes   Very.
Cross   Honest?
Gittes   As far as it goes. Of course he has to swim in the same water as we all do.
Cross   You may think you know what you're dealing with but believe me you don't. Why's that funny?
Gittes   That's what the District Attorney used to say to me in *Chinatown*.
Cross   Was he right? Exactly what do you know about me? Sit down.

Throughout the film, water is both creative and destructive. In the preceding conversation it has a polluted quality. At other points in the film, it is salt water at the Mulwray's house which kills the grass but also suggests to Gittes the truth of what is happening. At this point death and creative insight have become linked. Taking another example, near the start of the film, the photographs of Katherine and Hollis taken at a boating lake in Echo Park prompt Gittes to remark, 'Water again'. Later in the film, Hollis is found mysteriously drowned, in what is the middle of a drought.

One of the more curious and almost surreal moments in the film occurs as Gittes talks to a young boy who is riding a horse along a dried up riverbed. The scene is shot close to sunset, which gives the image a rich, warm, orange light. The whiteness of the horse and the detached air of the boy, together, give a sense of unreality to the scene. It is

Hollis Mulwray (Darrell Zwerling) talks to the boy on horseback (Claudio Martinz) *Chinatown*

here that Gittes learns that 'The water comes at different parts in the river. Every night a different part'. This is an unnatural river, one whose nocturnal activities give it a certain proximity to the unconscious. In the spirit of mythological amplification, it is interesting to note that in Greek mythology the sea god Poseidon created the horse. This indicates a strong association with the underworld of emotions. The sea and the horse are symbolically related and refer to passion; for example, waves are called 'white horses'. It is also possible to talk about bridling of passion. The boy on the horse on the riverbed is symbolic of the carrying of the child by the mother (or baby in the womb), hence, female libido or anima. Like the epic waters of Noah's flood, the water in *Chinatown* is destructive; unlike them it lacks any redemptive quality.

It is something of an interpretive convention in Jungian psychology that images of water are related to the unconscious. In the same way that a Freudian interpretation of symbols tends to reduce their meaning to sexuality, so too Jungian's have their own set of meanings and a distinct tendency to read symbolic images as in someway directly related to archetypal unconscious contents. Jung sets the trend. For our purposes, it is interesting that at several points he uses the metaphor of riverbeds to explain the function and the nature of archetypal structures.

> Archetypes are like riverbeds which dry up when the water deserts them, but which it can find again at any time. An archetype is like an old watercourse along which the water of life has flowed for centuries, digging a deep channel for itself. The longer it has flowed in the channel the more likely it is that sooner or later the water will return to its old bed.[6]

There are moments in *Chinatown* which seem curiously at odds with the general tone of the film's imagery. We have already begun to see how what appears to be straightforward denotive imagery (as in the film's use of photographic images) actually activates a mildly affective state in the viewer which manifests itself as a psychological discomfort. Alternately, and to use a more psychotherapeutic terminology, it is anxiety-provoking. The same is true of these more obviously, out-of-place images; the boy on horseback, visited on separate occasions by Hollis and Gittes is one such image as are the angry shepherds who release a flock of sheep into a committee room during a discussion about the proposed Alto Valley Vallejo dam. One way of thinking about this latter sequence is suggested by Len Masterman's 1970 article on Polanksi's film *Cul-de-sac* (1966), in which he notes Polanksi's observation, 'I must confess that I was completely formed by surrealism. Ten years ago, and even at the time when I was making my first shorts, I saw everything in the mirror of surrealism'.[7] Even though the films are almost a decade apart both have their surreal moments. Of course, Surrealists are well known for their interest in the unconscious and Salvador Dali's famous dream sequence for Hitchcock's *Spellbound* (1945) comes immediately to mind. To indulge in a little more amplification, if Noah Cross echoes the biblical Noah of Genesis then sheep suggest the passage from Isiah 53:6, 'All we like sheep have gone astray' and its associated following verse, 'like a lamb led to the slaughter' (Isiah 53:7). Innocence, be it of a lamb or human in a corrupt world, leads not to salvation but to destruction. To be clear, the suggestion here is emphatically not that something Christological is at stake

– the interest is not one of theology but of psychology. What is at play is some deep-rooted symbolism which suggests that something good, child-like and innocent is at risk of corruption.

This type of tension, in which two apparently opposing meanings in an image can also be thought of as releasing a third less immediately apparent meaning, is germane to imagery of the fish that occurs throughout the film. Normally symbols hold together opposing meanings, but there is nothing whole or containing in this imagery in *Chinatown*, and in this respect it is far removed, if suggestive, of the Christian symbol of the fish. A Christogram is a combination of letters which form either an abbreviation of the name of Christ or a related saying, as in IXQUS, (the letters in this case standing for Jesus, Christ, of God, Son Saviour and spelling – fish). But in *Chinatown* the images of fish are scattered throughout the film, somehow never quite managing to coalesce into a coherent symbol. For example, the fish which forms the logo of the Albacore Club is cut up, dismembered and turned into a quilt. Further, while it would be unwise to make too much of this, is it accidental that it is a fisherman who both opens the film and who plays a key role at the close of the narrative? What could be a key symbol and set of mythological motifs in the film fail to become so. Along with some of the film's more surreal moments the fragmented symbolic structure causes a state of uneasiness and at the end of the film we find out why.

Incest is always a disturbing matter, and so it is in *Chinatown*. At one level the film serves to point up the dreadful consequences of what can happen in actual cases. In this instance, it is made all the more distasteful when the audience learn that Evelyn was not coerced into having sex with her father but did so willingly. At this point it is important to deliteralize what is on screen. The Jungian term 'kinship libido' is to describe the psychological energy that flows between the archetypes in the unconscious of which the internal family is composed. To be clear, in no sense is Jung is referring to an outer-world, real family but rather his interest is with the internalized psychological images of father, mother, daughter and son that everyone carries within themselves. This is the archetypal family, not an actual bodily one. Of course, as with all archetypes, they can find themselves often unwittingly projected onto the outer world. At such times the danger exists that internal and external relationships become confused. Any such acting out of unconscious inner-world fantasies in the real world is bound to be disastrous.

The psychoanalytic view of fantasies of incest is well documented. Jung's views are less well known. In keeping with his theoretical position that libidinal energy is only in part sexual, he suggests that the internal incestuous fantasy can best be understood as a desire for rebirth, which is to say for psychological growth.

> One of the simplest ways [of finding someway into the mother's body] would be to impregnate the mother and beget oneself in identical from all over again. But here the incest prohibition intervenes; consequently the sun myths and rebirth myths devise every conceivable kind of mother-analogy for the purpose for *canalizing* the libido into new forms and effectively preventing it from regressing to actual incest. For instance, the mother is transformed into an animal, or is made young again, and

The Albacore Quilt *Chinatown*

then disappears after giving birth ie., is changed back into her old shape. It is not incestuous cohabitation that is desired, but rebirth. The incest prohibition acts as an obstacle and makes the creative fantasy inventive; for instance, there are attempts to make the mother pregnant by means of fertility magic. The effect of the incest-taboo and of the attempts at canalization is to simulate the creative imagination, which gradually open up possible avenues for the self-realization of the libido. In this way the libido becomes imperceptibly spiritualized. The power which 'always desires evil' thus creates spiritual life.[8]

At risk of providing an overly literal interpretation, it is nonetheless interesting that the riverbeds in *Chinatown* have run dry. It is only at night, presumably with the knowledge of Noah Cross, that that water is released. The cue to interpret this material as unconscious is provided by the juxtaposition of the boy on horseback with the dried up river course. The suggestion is that somehow the natural regulating function of the psyche has broken down. As in Shakespearian tragedy, or Arthurian myth, the state of the land reflects the state of its rulers. So too in *Chinatown* unnatural events in the landscape of the natural world mirror the disruption that is taking place in the unconscious and, specifically, in the interpersonal relationship between father and daughter.

Andrew Samuels goes one step further. In writing about kinship libido he suggests that it has the capacity to hold together relationships, forms and institutions. It is this potentially dangerous energy that also has the capacity to heal; it is at once both solvent and adhesive. From the opening moments of the film it is clear that social, cultural and institutional structures are breaking down. The sheep that invade in a formal hearing, during which the representative of the board of Water and Power refuses to build a dam, and the unmasking of Evelyn Mulwray's impostor all suggest that the political structures of life, which is to say the politics of the individual and of institutions, are dissolving. The reason for this is that the potentially cohesive energy of kinship libido has turned into something that is corrosive. Samuels comments,

Which aspects of psychology are most suggestive in relation to political change? What about unconscious fantasies of incestuous sexuality that drive the psychological relationships within the internal family...Critically examined, can kinship libido be socialised, that is, understood in broad terms as holding social organisms and political forms together? If so, different facets of kinship libido, different kinds of incestuous sexual fantasies, will be involved in the emergence and destruction of different political forms. At one point, Jung's hints that kinship libido helps to hold 'creeds, parties, nations or states together'.[9]

Jung does indeed make such a claim, at least in a manner of speaking. The passage which Samuels is alluding to can be found in Jung's article *The Psychology of the Transference*. Here he argues that while kinship libido may have a bonding role in the structures of society that this is not enough. For Jung, what matters is the relationship that exists to the Self within the psyche and to actual human relationships.

Everyone is now a stranger among strangers. Kinship libido – which could still engender a satisfying feeling of belonging together, as for instance in the early Christian communities – has long been deprived of its object. But, being an instinct, it is not to be satisfied by any mere substitute such as a creed, party, nation or state. It wants the *human* connection. That is the core of the whole transference phenomenon, and it is impossible to argue it away, because relationship to the self is at once relationship to our fellow man, and no one can be related to the latter until he is related to himself.[10]

In *Chinatown* this does not happen. Virtually no one appears to act in an honest, integrated and committed manner. An interesting exception is Jake, the fisherman who both starts and ends the film. The inability to separate inner and outer realities leads to the breaking of the incest taboo, a disruption in the natural order which is reflected as rivers dry up and corrupt political institutions operate for personal gain and not collective good. In this sense, the symbols in *Chinatown* fail to hold together these tensions. They suggest the possibility of wholeness and unity but are out of place in the predominately diurnal world of the film. *Chinatown* explores what happens when the human condition itself is corrupted. It is always impossible to separate out inner life of the unconscious from the realities of the outer world as, in a reflexive relationship, the one influences the other. The inability of the symbols of the film to hold these tensions results in the release of a disturbing type of affect and the result is a pervading sense of discomfort and anxiety.

The final section of the film finally takes viewers to *Chinatown*. Interestingly, for a moment, the opening shots of the location drop the pretence of the period setting as the neon lights of 1970s America fill the screen. The effect is enhanced by the discordant music whose non-diegetic quality breaks the bond between viewer and screen and in so doing provides another disruption to the coherence and stability of the narrative. Again, the natural order as embodied by the realism of the film suggests that any prospect of a happy ending is out of the question. The effect is a subtle and unsettling one

Chinatown at Night *Chinatown*

The film concludes quickly and somewhat ambiguously. Evelyn shoots her father in the arm before driving herself and Katherine to safety. The police fire and the sound of a car horn and the car coming to a halt tell us the shooting was fatal. So far as Katherine knows, Noah Cross is her grandfather. It is impossible to know how long that particular illusion will be perpetuated. The film's closing comments come from one of Gitte's partners who counsels, 'Forget it, Jake. It's *Chinatown*'.

By its end *Chinatown* as a film and *Chinatown* as a place have both become metaphors for the human condition. If the city of Los Angeles represents the daylight world of consciousness and rationality then the underworld of the unconscious finds its imagery in the city's *Chinatown*. This is a place that it is impossible to avoid and despite what others might say cannot be forgotten. Jung would go further: as *Chinatown* all too graphically shows, to forget that the unconscious has a role to play in our everyday lives would be a disaster.

Notes
1. Jung, C. G. (1930/50) *Collected Works* vol. 15. (London: Routledge and Kegan Paul), para. 137.
2. Jung, C. G. (1964/70) *Collected Works* vol. 10. (London: Routledge and Kegan Paul), para. 195.
3. Incidentally, the same device is used by Hitchcock as part of the opening of *North by Northwest*, where on that occasion the MGM lion is set against a lurid green background.
4. Jung, C. G. (1954/66) *Collected Works* vol. 16. (London: Routledge and Kegan Paul), para. 111.
5. *Ibid.*, para. 111.
6. Jung, C. G. (1964/70) *Collected Works*, vol. 10. (London: Routledge and Kegan Paul), para. 395.
7. Masterman, L., *Cul-de-sac: Through the Mirror of Surrealism. Screen* vol 11 number 9 p. 44 pp. 44–6.

8. Jung, C. G. (1956/67) *Collected Works* vol. 5. (London: Routledge and Kegan Paul), para. 332. Emphasis as original.
9. Samuels, A. *Politics on the Couch*. (London: Profile Books, 2001), pp. 66–7.
10. Jung, C. G. (1954/66) *Collected Works*, vol. 16. (London: Routledge and Kegan Paul) para. 445. Emphasis as original.

4

A Jungian Approach to Television

It is self-evident that cinema and television are different media both in the way they address their respective audiences and in how their audiences watch the content. In a curious way these pronounced differences mean that it is all too easy to overlook the consequences of each medium and the ways they make quite different psychological demands on their viewers. To put this another way, viewers use cinema and television in different ways and to different ends. This chapter will focus on how television is watched and used in our everyday lives where even the very notion of 'watching' suggests a certain attitude and relationship to the screen. Some of these themes will be developed in the following chapter in this section, which explores how television advertisers use psychological techniques and imagery to manipulate the responses and reactions of viewers. The final chapter in this section shifts focus to look at a specific television series, namely *Star Trek: The Next Generation* and in particular its view of human psychology and suggests that its somewhat ambiguous views about humankind may be a contributing factor in the longevity of this remarkable project.

Television, unlike cinema, is a domestic technology. The cinema as a public technology makes clear demands on us as an audience. It requires us to make an effort, to travel to a particular place at a set time, to sit quietly in semi-darkness in the midst of strangers as the film unfolds on-screen. By contrast, television makes no such claims on us; seemingly viewers control how they interact with it, not the other way around. Television permeates our domestic spaces, in the lounge, the kitchen, the study and even that most intimate of spaces – the bedroom, viewers don't have to travel far to get access to television programmes. The open all hours, 24/7 convenience-store approach adopted by television provides for its audiences a means of entertainment that could hardly make less demands.[1] Yet as we shall see it is the apparently undemanding nature of television programmes which in fact points us toward the complex relationship that television viewers have with the screen

That our relationship with television is a close and complex one is not controversial and the past forty years or so have seen the proliferation of studies about television.

Interestingly, while cinema theory readily adapted ideas from psychoanalysis, the same cannot be said for television studies. Here the main modes of analysis and engagement have been concerned with sociological studies of either production or reception, which is to say the production of television programmes and their subsequent effect, if any on individuals and social groups. The so-called effects debate continues to run and run with little by way of hard evidence to support either the beneficial or deleterious effects of watching television. Another significant body of work has concerned itself with television as an institution and examined issues of ownership and control, policy and regulation. A final area of concern has been with the analysis of actual television programmes themselves. Yet even here, and again unlike textual analysis in film and literature, little space has been found for psychoanalytically based modes of enquiry. Instead, either detailed textual quasi-literary readings, or sociologically based content analysis of news stories, for example, have proliferated.

The proposal is to take some of this work and to look at some of its findings but not from their original methodological perspective but from the view offered by analytical psychology. This should provide a fresh take on some familiar issues and help to tease out something of the underlying relationship audiences have with television. Naturally, this is a partial view of how viewers relate to and use television.

Why do we watch TV?
The question of why anyone watches television at all is not a trivial one, and, indeed, it lies beneath much of what this chapter is about. It is by no means self-evident that viewers 'should' watch television and there are many other options, even in the field of audio-visual entertainment. Yet television continues to be the most popular, or at least readily consumed, of the mass media. In the UK most people make daily use of the media and broadly similar patterns are found in other countries. In a typical week: 94 per cent of the UK population (aged 4+) watch any TV; 90 per cent of the UK population (aged 15+) listen to any radio; 50 per cent of the UK population (aged 15+) read a daily national newspaper.[2] The assumption must be that the media, and in particular television, have some meaning for viewers in their everyday lives and that it is possible for television to be more than 'just' electronic wallpaper One possible explanation lies in the role television has as a purveyor of symbolic material. As Goethals commented back in 1980:

> As we approach the end of the twentieth century the mass media, especially television, have emerged as major conveyors of public symbols. Television has woven a web of myths, furnishing the rhythms, the visual extravaganzas, and pseudo-liturgical season that break up the ordinariness of our lives. It is a primary source of orientation to the social, political, and economic spheres of experience. Although television may have its greatest impact on those who rely on it as a primary source of news and entertainment, its environment of symbols surrounds us all.[3]

Of course, there are many reasons and motivations for watching television – many of them not concerned with the intricacies of symbols and myth-making and equally there is a wide range of emotions that can be attached to the experience. Guilt in watching day-time television, companionship, control and power concerning who watches what and when, not to mention emotional responses to the content of the programmes themselves. Such viewer behaviour is of interest to broadcasters for a number of reasons. Audience data provides a pecking order for the success, or otherwise, of different television companies. Commercial broadcasters need to provide such data to advertisers while public service broadcaster also too need to be able to reassure themselves that they are satisfying their remits. Content regulators are interested in who is watching what and when, for other equally pragmatic reasons.

As might be imagined, there is steadily growing mountain of research in this area. Recently much of this complex interaction has been captured in a longitudinal audience tracking study commissioned by the British Film Institute (BFI) and written up by David Gauntlett and Annette Hill (*TV Living: Television, Culture and Everyday Life*. BFI: London, 1999). Using a range of sociological approaches the book explores issues such as television and the organization of our daily lives, news, gender, violence and importantly television personal change and social interaction. Of particular interest is the evidence around the way that television is consciously used to facilitate social interaction and self-awareness. As the authors note:

> It is also possible that this respondent gained insight about her relationship through watching certain types of TV programmes. For example, when discussing talk shows, this woman wrote: 'They can be used to assist in discovery about relationship/gender issues and can be helpful if seen in conjunction with talking to real people in everyday life'.[4]

Interestingly, and perhaps predictably, television can also be used in quite the opposite manner, as a way of evading issues. In the following extract, the use of television shifts from specific types of programmes which might facilitate a sense of self-discovery to the act of watching television. Here watching becomes a type of displacement activity.

> In the recent past, TV was such a ritual and a crutch to a failing relationship. It provided so many ways of evading 'real' conversation – especially from me. It was like a passive third party to the relationship.[5]

Or course, it is entirely possible that television has just been randomly selected as scapegoat here as there are many ways of evading 'real' conversations in a relationship. But it is significant that watching television as a couple, as a joint activity, became a symbol for their lack of unity. The final use that Gauntlett and Hill identified was the use of television programmes to facilitate social interaction as in this comment from a 14-year-old schoolgirl, where, as the authors note, the pleasure of the programme is clearly bound up with anticipation of subsequent discussion.

> My all time favourite programmes include *Cracker* [detective series set in Scotland] because it is very exciting and because it's always coming up in conversation the next day.[6]

Or this comment from a 44-year-old female medical secretary.

> Sometimes in the office we tell each other what's happening in our favourite soaps if, for example one of us has missed an episode. We have also talked about particularly interesting programmes e.g. *Forty Minutes* [documentary strand], *Inside Story* [documentary strand] and a few watch *Making Out* [drama series].

It is worth noting that the majority of the comments in this section of *TV Living* come from women. There is some evidence to suggest that men also use television programmes to facilitate similar types of discussions but these tend to be based around sport rather than soap operas or documentaries.

As a sociological document *TV Living* is clearly of benefit in providing actual accounts of the uses to which people put television, or, at least, the claims they make about their uses. As such it is a most welcome addition and as a longitudinal study it will continue to provide a rich source of information over the coming years. It confirms the wide range of uses to which people put television in their everyday lives. Offering far more than just entertainment, television is actively used by its viewers to facilitate social interchange as a means for greater self-understanding. However, based as it is around such empirical data it does not look at the broader issues around television. Indeed, surprisingly little has been written about this area other than from the perspective offered by the media effects debates. What follows is an attempt to explore some of the general psychological uses to which television is put by its viewers. To do so it is necessary to move away from an empirical sociological approach and to try and locate television as a technology and to regard watching television programmes as cultural activity.

The starting point for the following psychological speculation may seem a little curious, originating as it does in cultural theory. Yet the suggestion is that Raymond Williams' proposition that cinema and television programmes exist not as discrete and separate entities but instead can more usefully be seen as part of a planned 'flow' of programmes has a psychological relevance. Williams was keen to stress that while television is made up of separate elements (individual programmes) and sub-elements (the visual structures within each programme) that it was the sequence of programmes that was of significance. Just as the visual composition of each television programme is designed to attract the viewer, so to is the flow of one programme to the next.

> Analysis of a distribution of interest or categories in a broadcasting programme, while in its own terms significant, is necessarily abstract and static. In all developed broadcasting systems the characteristic organisation, and therefore the characteristic experience, is one of sequence or flow. This phenomenon, of planned flow, is then perhaps the defining characteristic of broadcasting, simultaneously as a technology and as a cultural form.[7]

Central to his analysis is the way in which programme 'flows' into another. Here he suggests that trailers for other programmes, either that day or later in the week, create the suggestion that any given television channel's programmes should just unfold on the screen. Writing as he was in the 1970s, this was quite an insight. Nowadays media savvy viewers are wise to the wily ways of the television scheduler. They know how programme time-slots are horizontally stripped across the week's viewing with the same programme at the same time each day. They understand that broadcasters need to deliver viewers for their advertisers and would rather viewers sit and watch their channel all evening rather just 'cherry-pick' the programmes they want to watch. Yet there is something compelling about Williams' observation that programmes flow, even in a multi-channel age. John Ellis sums up Williams' position succinctly:

> According to William's flow model, then, everything becomes rather like everything else, units are not organised into coherent single texts like cinema films, but form a kind of montage without overall meaning.[8]

Readers familiar with the current state of UK television will recognize a state of affairs that could not unreasonably be described as 'a montage without overall meaning'. As one home makeover programme merges into the next, as one reality television format follows hard on the heels of another, and as home shopping channels peddle their wares might indeed seem that television is without meaning.

Of course, viewers can resist this attraction. In theory there is nothing to stop us looking at the schedule and deciding if there is a programme we want to watch. The television does not have to be switched on the moment we walk through the door as a way of forgetting about the concerns of the day. Indeed, there are some signs that this way of watching television may be on the increase. Technologies such as Sky+ which enable viewers to record onto a hard drive in the decoder box, also track television viewing habits. Based on viewing patterns the equipment will automatically record programmes that might prove of interest. Notwithstanding issues of surveillance and privacy, the technology offers the potential, at least, for more selective patterns of viewing. Whether this happens is, of course, another matter, and broadcasters will be keen to make sure that any such development does not result in the loss of advertising revenue, which is central to the existence of commercial television.

John Ellis also helpfully makes the distinction between watching television and watching television programmes. He notes that the first refers to the unfolding and ceaseless flow of continuous television, day and night while the latter separates out the targeting viewing of specific television programmes, although this remains an unusual way of watching television. Ellis develops this thought into a more general theory about the nature of the different modes of address that each medium adopts towards its audience. Here he takes something of a departure from the mainstream of television theory and uses the psychoanalytic notion of 'the look' to distinguish between the realms of spectatorship in the cinema and the glance or casual look of the television viewer.

> TV's regime of vision is less intense than cinema's: it is a regime of the glance rather than the gaze. The gaze implies a concentration of the spectator's activity into that of looking, the glance implies that no extraordinary effort is being invested in the

activity of looking...The cinema looker is a spectator: caught by the projection yet separate from its illusion. The TV-looker is a viewer, casting a lazy eye over proceedings, keeping an eye on events. In psychoanalytic terms, when compared to cinema, TV demonstrates a displacement from the invocatory drive of scopophilia (looking) to the closest related of the invocatory drives, that of hearing. Hence the crucial role of sound in ensuring continuity of attention and producing the utterances of direct address ('I' to 'you').[9]

Ellis may well be right to emphasize the normally casual nature of watching television. He is also right to draw our attention to the importance of sound (an aspect of television that is often overlooked) as it is this which keeps viewers informed of what is happening on the screen, even if they are not directly looking at it. In using the term 'invocatory drive', Ellis may have had in mind Christian Metz's 1975 article *The Passion for Perceiving*[10] in which Metz makes the distinction between the scopic drive (the desire to see which manifests itself in voyeurism and scopophilia) and the '*pulsion invocante*', the desire to hear – the invocatory drive. Metz observes these two sexual drives are closer to the imaginary than other drives precisely because they maintain their object at a distance – the distance of the look and distance of listening. While Metz was writing about cinema, his observations are a neat fit with Ellis' view of the television viewer in which the power of the gaze is depleted and replaced with a somewhat feeble gaze or, as he puts it, a glance.

> Broadcast TV recruits the interest of its viewers by creating a complicity of viewing: the TV look at the world becomes a surrogate look for the viewers. TV presents the events of the world, both documented and imagined, to an audience that is secure at home, relaxing and seeking diversion. Broadcast TV creates a community of address in which viewer and TV institution both look at a world that exists beyond them both...Hence the lack of a truly voyeuristic position for the TV viewer. It is not the TV viewer's gaze that is engaged, but his or her glance, a look without power.[11]

This emasculation extends beyond the realm of the scopic regime and Ellis suggests that it renders the television viewer in a state of complicity. The power of the look is delegated, or transferred, to the television set. The 'window-on-the-world' is invested with the power of the gaze as responsibility for 'looking' is devolved from the self to the television screen. This disinvests the viewer of any sense of social agency and leaves them isolated and powerless.

> The effect for the viewer of this processes of delegation of the look to TV is rather unexpected. TV tends to assume that this delegation enables it to function as the surrogate of its viewers, seeing for them, seeing into them to provide both information and entertainments. However, the process is rather less certain. The process of delegation of the look leaves the TV viewer in a position of isolation rather than separation from the events shown. The sense of complicity with the audience presented by broadcast TV tends to intensify this isolation.[12]

However, in this somewhat bleak view of the television viewer there is a tension which offers some hope. While the invocatory drive may hold its object at a distance, the notion of invocation suggests an attraction. The Latin *vocare* means to call. In common English usage an invocation suggests a summons, the summoning of a spirit though charms and spells. When we impose this interpretive frame on the viewer-screen relationship we recast it in quite a different light. One which suggests that the processes do not solely consist of isolation and complicity (although it can) but may also activate an unconscious psychological process in which something from within viewers is drawn forth. Less dramatically, the process seems to fit well with the psychological mechanisms of transference and identification as images and sounds of television programmes have the capacity to release unconscious processes which enable viewers to relate to television in a complex manner.

This suggests different types of psychological engagement occur in the act of watching television and in the activity of watching television programmes. Watching a television programme suggests a relationship more akin that of the cinemagoer watching a film. The screen is the immediate and dominant object of interest, the relationship is participatory and relatively unconscious (closer to the dream state, as Metz might put it). In contrast the watcher of television is bathed in the invocatory flow of images and sounds. The programme maybe on 'in the background', the 'viewer' may even be in a different room following only in a subliminal manner whatever is on the television.

In psychoanalytic film studies, this type of argument has been used to advance the importance of film as the medium with the greatest psychological impact, partly because of its claimed proximity to the dream state. The large screen, the relaxed warm room (like a bedroom, so it goes), the identification with the screen (taking what is on-screen as being almost real), all contribute to the dream-like experience of watching a film. That viewers have involuntary body movements both while watching a film and dreaming again is suggestive of similarity at a somatic level between the two activities.

Yet it is possible to adopt another quite different perspective on the viewer-screen relationship in which immersive identificatory qualities are not so significant. It has already been argued that television as a domestic technology which competes for the viewer's attention with other occurrences in the house is less involving than cinema. The relatively small screen also makes it less immersive than cinema. Perhaps curiously, this relative lack of identification with television programmes does not necessarily leave this process as a-psychological. In fact, the repetitive nature of television, the flow of television to use Williams' terminology and its 'always on' quality, offers the potential for another type of psychological relationship.

It is this 'always on' quality that takes us back to the relationship between dreams and other images. Perhaps the ways that dreams are understood, or interpreted, might also shed some light on how to understand the flow of television. James Hillman in his book *The Dream and the Underworld* suggests that it is a mistake to worry too much about the interpretation of dreams. Instead, he suggests that what is important is to experience the dream, time and time again – to let the imagery of the dream sit in front of the individual. Hillman's claim is that just the actual experience of the image is enough to effect psychological transformation.

From the comparison of dreams with myth, healing cult, and religious mysteries, we can understand that changes take place in participants even without direct interpretative intervention. It is not about what is said about the dream after the dream, but the experience of the dream after the dream...This implies to me that dreams can be killed by interpreters, so that the direct application of the dream as a message for the ego is probably less effective in actually changing consciousness and affecting life than is the dream still kept alive as an enigmatic image.[13]

It is possible that this rather grandiose view of psychological reality and its potentially transformative qualities might seem somewhat removed from the reality of everyday television. Surely, the seemingly unending flow of reality television, lifestyle makeovers and home improvement programmes has little, if anything, to do with the richness of our inner psychological lives. Perhaps Goethals expression of a similar sentiment, but in a less technical vocabulary, makes the point:

Through the ritual and iconic richness of its visual images, television answers, at least in part, those sacramental needs [of people]. Its images offer the security of real or imagined 'worlds' larger than the individual. And at the same time they hold out to viewers, perhaps not the reality of heroism, but the excitement of vicarious human adventure. To live today in the awareness of a mystical, transcendent order of being and of unknown dimensions of time and human experience opens up fearful and undreamed-of worlds. These realities are frightening, for they awaken us from sleep we had not known as sleep. It is much easier to pull the covers of culture over our heads and sleep a little longer before awakening. It is much easier to watch the world turn on soaps and stay tuned to the Super Bowl.[14]

However, it is necessary to part company with Hillman and Goethals. Firstly, it must be recognized that people choose to watch a whole range of television programmes. This would seem to suggest that something beneficial is being found in these programmes and this could be a psychological benefit. Nor does it seem reasonable to suggest that people watch television because they do not know any better. Instead, perhaps the decision as to what is watched, and when and how, comes about from the unconscious dynamics in play at any given moment. Both watching television and television programmes may help in connecting to the reality of given situation. This, suggests Jung, is the function of dream imagery – to state the psychological situation as it is.

...the dream comes in as the expression of an involuntary, unconscious psychic process beyond the control of the conscious mind. It shows the inner truth and reality of the patient as it really is: not as I conjecture it to be, and as he would like it to be, but *as it is*....I take dreams as diagnostically valuable facts.[15]

While Jung puts the image centre-stage in coming to a view about the psychological reality of a situation in one of his intriguing, and sometimes infuriating, moments, he flips the situation on its head and suggests the opposite might also be true. This type of running together of opposites (what Jung terms *enantiodromia*) is actually one of the founding principals of the psyche. Opposites do not necessarily contradict or pull each other apart. Rather, for Jung, opposites may eventually, somehow, come together. While Jung was not referring to television, nonetheless, the following quote gives us quite a different view of the psychological relevance of images – one which seems germane to our understand of the popular psychological appeal of television, and one which provides the potential for a positive approach to the viewer's relationship to television.

> Although, as a rule, no reality-value attaches to the image, this can at times actually increase its importance for psychic life, since it then has a greater *psychological* value, representing an inner reality which often far outweighs the importance of external reality.[16]

From this perspective it can be seen that the image *per se* is not what is important. The most significant factor is the psychic (for which read psychological) value that is attached to the image. Television programmes, even reality television, actually have little to do with the real world. Soap operas, for all their pretence, are not about real people in real situations, and as viewers we know that to be the case. In the media-literate, postmodern savvy world viewers also know that all television programmes are mediated and that they feed off each other through a complex system of inter-textual references and connections. While there are ways in which television programmes respond to and meet inner psychological needs, perhaps just having the need met is not enough as it also needs to be understood and evaluated. To do this it is necessary to understand what part of the unconscious self is being met by watching television. However, the dissolution of the unconscious processes that structure our relationship with 'the image' is not an easy process. As Hillman puts it:

> Taking back projections in practice is not as simple as it sounds, since to dissolve a projection is to lose body, to lose that vessel where what matter has been placed. Such projections are like fixed or overvalued ideas. They have delusional quality, because they cannot be seen through as psychic fixations and psychic values.[17]

The evocation of television programmes as 'fixed or overvalued ideas' seems right. Daytime television in the UK consistently offers the promise of ways of living a better life. Nutritionists offer advice about our diets (without knowing what we actually eat), interior designers suggest ways our home can be improved (without knowing what it looks like), and the lives of others less fortunate than ourselves are offered for our inspection and sometimes comment. It presents a curious mixture of how our life could be better and also how it might also be worse. All this serves to stimulate in us a curious narcissistic fascination with ourselves which offers little by way of actual insight. After all, how could it? This is mass television, not individual therapy. Yet if a way could be found in which it was possible to find a space, time and process for reflection, then this might reveal the psychological values with which we are concerned.

In trying to breakdown the defences of consciousness it is sometimes a good idea to sneak up on the problem from behind. More technically, this is an attempt at a circumambulation of the defences of consciousness as a technique by which to explore a psychological complex. In this spirit, perhaps there is something about the fundamental nature of electronic communication that might be informative. One of the best-known commentators on the development of modern electronic communication is Marshall McLuhan, and he is widely credited as coining the term 'global village'. His article *The Medium is the Message* was published in 1964, and its prescient quality has led to its appeal to readers in the age of the Internet. As in much of his writing, McLuhan clearly intended the piece to have a strong psychological quality (it ends with a quote from Jung)[18] although this aspect is often overlooked in favour of its central concern with content and medium (note, not form and content) and the notion he espouses of the technological extension of humankind. Of particular interest is his claim that the rise of technology means we live in a mythological age.

> In the mechanical age now receding, many actions could be taken without too much concern. Slow movement insured that the reactions were delayed for considerable periods of time. Today the action and the reaction occur almost at the same time. We actually live mythically and integrally, as it were, but we continue to think in the old, fragmented space and time patterns of the pre-electric age.[19]

McLuhan is trying to suggest that communication is now so fast it is almost part of who we are – it is almost an extension of ourselves – and there is something 'magical' about this rate of change that our psyche has still not adjusted to. To anyone familiar with Jung, this is a little difficult to come to terms with. Jung was not at all convinced about the redemptive role of technology; in fact, he held quite the opposite point of view. (Chapter Six takes a detailed look at this issue.) Where McLuhan and Jung might agree is that there is discrepancy between our psychological heritage (old space and time patterns) and our current cultural condition, this is partly characterized by a desire to live mythically and integrally; which is to say in a holistic manner. McLuhan comes back to this idea in *Media Hot and Cold* noting:

> Today, deep in the electric age, organic myth is itself a simple and automatic response capable of mathematical formulation and expression...For myth *is* the instant vision of a complex process that ordinarily extents over a long period. Myth is contraction or implosion of any process, and the instant speed of electricity confers the mythic dimension on ordinary industrial and social action today. We *live* mythically but continue to think fragmentarily and on single planes.[20]

To unpick this a little McLuhan seems to be suggesting that myth is something which can happen in an instant; it is the contraction of complicated lengthy histories into a compressed moment. As far as analytical psychology is concerned, myths are essentially symbolic acts, images, narratives and so forth which give expression to unconscious ideas and processes. As such they exist outside time. If time is of any relevance then mythic time is certainly different to our regular perception of our everyday linear time. Mythic time can be slow, cyclical and certainly elastic. So when McLuhan comments that we live mythically but continue to think on single planes this could be reinterpreted in psychological terminology to mean that we experience life mythically, but we are not conscious of this; or to invert the statement we are unconscious of our mythological engagement with the world.

McLuhan suggests that technology is one of our modern myths. It is unusual to think of technology as mythological as normally it is located firmly within a modernist, post-industrial revolution materialist discourse. Yet as explored above, television is only partly concerned with the real world. In fact, it has the potential to reconnect us to another aspect of our lives in which we see things more symbolically, ritualistically or, as McLuhan might put it, mythologically. In his definition of technology, he defines each medium as either hot or cold. Here again is another interesting paradox which on the surface does not appear to make much sense. Hot media are high definition, i.e. they are full of information, or data, while by contrast a cold medium is low definition. In his article *Media Hot and Cold*, he puts it as follows:

> There is a basic principle that distinguishes a hot medium like radio from a cool one like the telephone, or a hot medium like the movie from a cool one like TV. A hot medium is one that extends one single sence in 'high definition.' High definition is the state of being well filled with data. A photograph is, visually, 'high definition'. A cartoon is 'low definition,' simply because very little information is provided...Any hot medium allows of less participation than a cool one, as a lecture makes for less participation than a seminar, and book for less than dialogue.[21]

Of course, this categorization of media as either hot or cold can only be partially successful. In the extract above, speech as a medium is both hot (when in a lecture) and cold (when in a seminar), context, then, also effects the temperature of the medium. But it is interesting that lower definition media offer the opportunity for a greater degree of participation than hot media. Within the terms of this framework, television is cool medium as it is fairly low resolution and takes place in the domestic environment with plenty of opportunity for the viewer's interaction with the programme and the home environment. Now if participation is thought of in psychological and mythological terms, it is possible to suggest that, in fact, it is the very low definition, on in the background, present in the home qualities of television which contribute to its psychological value. Its low resolution qualities enable the projection of inner unconscious dynamics even though we are not aware that we are living in a mythological manner. To use the language of depth psychology as viewers, we are unconscious of how the images and sounds in our lives effect our everyday interactions and of the potential they have to speak to our inner selves. To describe this lack of consciousness, McLuhan writes about the principle of numbness which is induced by technology:

> We have to numb our central nervous system when it is extended and exposed, or we will die. Thus the age of anxiety and of electric media is also the age of the unconscious and of apathy. But it is strikingly the age of consciousness of the unconscious, in addition. With our central nervous system strategically numbed, the tasks of conscious awareness and order are transferred to the physical life of man, so that for the first time he has become aware of technology as an extension of his physical body. Apparently this could not have happened before the electric age gave us the means of instant, total field-awareness.[22]

So again another apparent contradiction as apparently as it is important to be numb to the effects of electric media but at the same time the electric age provides us with instant total field-awareness. From the perspective of depth psychology it is important to focus on the metaphor of the body that McLuhan employs. The image of numbness that he uses is a type of defence mechanism by which the body protects itself from harm. But what if instead of positioning technology as extension of the physical body it is seen as an extension of the psychological self? In so doing numbness becomes the expression of a psychological complex, a fear of being overwhelmed by the unconscious. People in states of psychological shock often report not feeling anxious or terrified or even depressed but rather they describe themselves 'numb'. In the image-saturated world we live in, a cultural compensation from the unconscious is there to provide the opportunity to reconnect to our inner selves.

The task seems daunting. Perhaps some reassurance can be found in Jung's view that within every individual there exist numerous psychological complexes which have the tendency to split away from the unconscious and which appear to operate as individual personalities. In other words, this process is quite normal and natural.

> ...the manifestations of the unconscious do a least show *traces of personalities*. A simple example is the dream, where a number of real or imaginary people represent the dream-thoughts. In nearly all the important types of dissociation, the manifestations of the unconscious assume a strikingly personal form. Careful examination of the behaviour and mental content of these personifications, however, reveals their fragmentary character. They seem to represent complexes that have split off from a greater whole, and are the very reverse of a personal centre of the unconscious.[23]

Perhaps the multi-channel world of television is not unlike the fragmented, disassociated state of our contemporary psychological life. If so, then television and other image-making technologies while remaining the product of rationalism and industrial society actually serve the psychological purposes of providing us with new ways of making, sharing and experiencing images; those same images which are the very centre of the psyche. This should not be so surprising as, after all, sound and image as invocation and symbol are at the heart of mythological life. The puzzle is why our cultural insistence on literalizing the imagery we produce. If Jung is right about the psychological principle of compensation, until society comes to realize the psychological function and qualities of the images with which it is surrounded, the psyche will continue their production at ever-increasing rates. Put simply, despite what our rational minds might tell us, television, the Internet and film are new mythologies; they are new symbolic media and the challenge is to find the right myths, the meaningful myths through which to better understand our lives. In his article *The Spirit in the Tube*, Schenk puts it in the following manner:

> We have found that, seen through psychological vision, television is a world encompassing us with a life of its own. Following alchemy and Jung, I am suggesting that the intention of this life is to unite spirit or invisible life with material or visible life to make psychological 'image'.[24]

This observation neatly makes the distinction between television as self-contained world (in other words, not directly related to the real world) and the interaction that viewers have with television; the way in which this process can offer the opportunity for a psychological understanding of ourselves, our relationships and the culture at large. Part of this is to use symbols and myths as part of the processes of making unconscious meaning conscious. However, equally important to the psychological mode is the act of reflecting and evaluating on the values attributed to such mythologies. This provides a means through which projections can be withdrawn and the complexes that have been projected onto the outer world integrated into our psychological selves. The practice of connecting everyday life with another view of reality is, of course, an inherently mythological activity. Trying to see in the images that surround us aspects of our conscious and unconscious selves requires us to become more conscious of who we are, not just what life has turned us into. There are various psychological labels that can be given to this process – Jung called it 'individuation'.

Having suggested that television represents a new mythology, the next two chapters will explore two ways in which television recycles old myths. The first of these explores the use that advertising makes of the myth of Narcissus and the imagery of alchemy. The aim is to draw attention to how advertising draws on deep-seated anxieties about identity and the possibility of personal transformation and invests the products that it is promoting with these qualities. The final chapter in this section looks in detail at some episodes from *Star Trek: The Next Generation* that are particularly concerned with mental health. Far from seeing the futuristic universe of this series as a utopia, it examines the deep ambivalence that lies at the heart of the series about the true qualities of human nature. The issues that surround the role of technology, and particularly audio-visual technologies, will resurface once again in the chapter *Technology as Modern Myth and Magic*, which takes another look at the origins of contemporary attitudes to communication technologies and suggests that by adopting a psychological attitude it is possible to find other and rather different meanings.

Notes

1. A caveat concerns watching films at home, which is a different matter. Those large screens, which offer us the simulation of the 'real thing' are clearly popular. Manufacturers of liquid crystal or plasma displays along with hi-fi surround-sound makers have welcomed the public's acceptance of this technology. That at a time when technology is generally getting smaller and more portable, television moves in the opposite direction with multi-speaker systems, digital signal processors and massive, if thin, screens. But this is not watching television at all. This is watching film; it's the attempt to recreate the cinematic experience.
2. Based on data from BARB (Broadcasters Audience Research Board), NRS (National Readership Survey) and RAJAR (Radio Joint Audience Research). Data for week ended 17 April 2005.
3. Goethals, G. *The TV Ritual: Worship at the Video Altar.* (Boston: Beacon Press, 1981), p. 142.
4. Gauntlett, D., and Hill, A. *TV Living: Television, Culture and Everyday Life.* (London: BFI, 1999), p. 105.

5. *Ibid.*, p. 106.
6. *Ibid.*, p. 128.
7. Williams, R. *Television: Technology and Cultural Form.* (Lonodon: Schocken Books, 1975), p. 86.
8. Ellis, J. *Visible Fictions: Cinema, Television, Video.* (London: Routledge, 1982), p. 117.
9. *Ibid.*, p. 137.
10. Metz, C. *Psychoanalysis and Cinema: The Imaginary Signifier,* (London, Macmillan,1982), Heath, S., and MacCabe, C., *The Passion for Perceiving* originally published 1975, *Communications* 23.
11. Ellis, J. *Visible Fictions: Cinema, Television, Video,* (London: Routledge, 1982), p. 163.
12. Ellis, J., *Visible Fictions: Cinema, Television, Video,* (London: Routledge, 1982). p164.
13. Hillman, J. *The Dream and the Underworld,* (New York: Harper and Row, 1979), p. 122.
14. Goethals, G. *The TV Ritual: Worship at the Video Altar.* (Boston: Beacon Press, 1981), p. 143.
15. Jung, C. G. (1954/66) *Collected Works,* vol. 16. (London: Routledge and Kegan Paul), para. 304. Emphasis as original.
16. Jung, C. G. (1964/71) *Collected Works,* vol. 6. (London: Routledge and Kegan Paul), para. 744. Emphasis as original.
17. Hillman, J. *The Dream and the Underworld,* (New York: Harper and Row, 1979), p. 139.
18. McLuhan references the quote as *Contributions to Analytical Psychology,* London, 1928, a title which does not appear in the standard Collected Works. The quote appears to be the same as a passage in *Women in Europe* (1927/1929) CW10:249.
19. McLuhan, M. *Understanding Media: The Extensions of Man.* (Cambridge, Massachusetts: MIT Press, 1995), p. 4.
20. *Ibid.*, p. 25. Emphasis as original.
21. *Ibid.*, pp. 22–23.
22. *Ibid.*, p. 47.
23. Jung, C. G. (1959/68) *Collected Works,* vol. 9i. (London: Routledge and Kegan Paul), para. 507. Emphasis as original.
24. Schenk, R. 'The Spirit in the Tube: The Life of Television' in Brooke, R. (ed.) *Pathways into the Jungian World: Phenomenology and Analytical Psychology.* (London: Routledge, 2000), p. 100.

5

Narcissism and the Alchemy of Advertising

Introduction

Many media academics, perhaps most, will find the title of this chapter a little eccentric; at worst it might appear ludicrous. On the other hand, Jungian analysts, depending on the their preferences, might be less surprised. The question, which naturally springs to mind, is what possible link could there be between alchemy and advertising? After all, the world of alchemy, with its dubious claims to transform lead into gold, is surely nothing like modern-day advertising, is it? The connection, if indeed there is one, is not to be taken in a causal sense. Rather, this chapter explores the subtle interplay between the imagery and intent of alchemy, and the psychologically charged images used in television adverts. (This is not to imply that print advertisements are devoid of psychological imagery, just that they are not our immediate object of concern.) Perhaps it is self-evident that advertising actively feeds a cultural preoccupation with self-image defined in terms of ownership of products. More curious are the ways in which modern capitalist values derive, in part, their power from the myth of Narcissus – what is found in advertising is an interesting interweaving of the ideological and the archetypal. Perhaps this should not be too much of a surprise; after all, advertising sets out to promote an awareness of products and to suggest how they might improve our everyday life.

Traditional Approaches

A consideration of television advertising is generally approached from either business studies (marketing, public relations and so on) or from the perspectives that broadly fall into what we might call media studies. Curiously, media studies has not paid too much attention to television adverts and historically most of the work in this area has focused on magazine advertising (Williamson 1978, Dyer 1982, Myers 1982, Alvarado and Thompson [eds] 1990), although most of these texts do make *some* reference to television advertising. More recently Renèe Dickason has produced a useful account of the historical development of advertising on British television, but her focus is on forms and institutions rather than the actual advertisements they produce.

In the earliest of these pieces, Williamson's analysis of advertising uses what is a broadly semiological method. *Decoding Advertisements* is in three parts. The first is dedicated to establishing the sign-signifier relations and the hermeneutic conventions that are deployed in trying to understand an advert. The second part where Williamson develops what she refers to as 'ideological castles: Referent Systems' is of more interest. Taking her cue from Lévi-Strauss, one of the chapters in this section is titled 'Cooking Nature'. (Cf. Claude Lévi-Strauss, *The Raw and the Cooked: Introduction to a Science of Mythology*, Random House: London, 1969.) This points to one of the central concerns of her book, namely the way that advertising draws on cultural myths of transformation. Williamson suggests that advertisers produce images that have been derived from the natural world and that these images are subsequently 'cooked' (i.e. imbued with contemporary cultural association, and in so doing naturalized) with the intention of producing desirable goods. The biological metaphor of consumption seems apt. However, what is important in this sleight of hand is that while the process appears to the consumer to be natural it is in reality heavily institutionalized and ideological.

Chapter 6 of Williamson's book focuses on magic and particularly on the themes of transformation, incantation, spells and alchemy: themes that we will return to and enlarge on in the following exploration of television advertisements. Williamson suggests that these themes are potent myths that are put to work by advertisers and that they are effective in concealing the capitalist power relations that exist between producer and consumer, and which delude the consumer into a false sense of control and autonomy. For Williamson:

> Magic is the production of results disproportionate to the effort put in (a transformation of power – or of impotence *into* power)...Magic can therefore be used to misrepresent any system of production...This is clearly analogous to the negation in ideology of the actual system of production in society.[1]

Williamson helpfully draws attention to the way in which magical images in advertising conceal the true nature of the production processes. Images of food being prepared apparently for each individual customer conceal the true conditions of its production, while at the same time purporting to document its creation. Actual factories are a rarity. Equally scarce are ingredients, or machine parts, while chemical preservatives and e-numbers are quite definitely a foreign territory for television advertisers. Nor are the actual conditions under which food is produced and harvested something that finds its way into advertisements. When images of food production are seen, they are of lush tea and coffee plantations, of tropical island paradises and sun-kissed cornfields which leave to one side the politics and production practices which are endemic to the food supply chain. Williamson goes on to argue that not only does magic lie in the ability of advertisements to conceal the material conditions of the production process it also appears to put the consumer in control. This illusion is created through making the consumer, in part, a magician.

But the only thing we can *do* in fact is to buy the product or incant its name – this is all the action possible as *our* part of the excitement offered. Such minimal action inevitably creates a 'magic spell' element: from a little action, we get 'great' results (or are promised them).[2]

For her, magic is not invested with psychological properties, rather it represents a distortion of the material world. She argues that 'Magic is therefore a kind of pivot around which misrepresentations may be produced'.[3] The key misrepresentation takes place in an intertwining of time and space through which time is incorporated into space. (A magic mirror lets you see into the future, or objects appear from nowhere.) In this sense she claims that all consumer products offer magic, and all advertisements cast spells. Some advertisements go even further and directly address themes of magic and the supernatural as they 'assume a system of transformation where such disproportionate results appear, miraculously...'.[4] It is interesting to remind ourselves that Williamson was writing in the 1970s and it might well have been the case that what she was identifying in advertising was nothing more than a passing fad; after all, advertising is notoriously trend-driven in its imagery. But, in fact, contemporary television advertising is redolent with such imagery and it has become institutionalized and is now part of the everyday visual vocabulary of the advertising industry.

The point is amplified by Raymond Williams in his seminal essay, *Advertising: the Magic System*, in which he provides a cogent analysis of the role of advertising in a capitalist society. His historical overview concludes by noting that

> It is impossible to look at modern advertising without realising that the material object being sold is never enough: this indeed is the crucial cultural quality of its modern forms...it is clear that we have a cultural pattern in which the objects are not enough but must be validated, if only in fantasy, by association with social and personal meanings which in a different cultural pattern might be more directly available. The short description of the pattern we have is *magic*: a highly organized and professional system of magical inducements and satisfactions, functionally very similar to magical systems in simpler societies, but rather strangely coexistent with a highly developed scientific technology.[5]

Without disagreeing with this perhaps something else is also happening. What neither Williams or Williamson examine is the psychological significance of this 'magical' imagery and the interesting theme that emerges – the desire to be a magician. This is something that is clearly stimulated by the imagery of television advertising, and it seems to appeal to a fundamental need which can be thought of as an archetypal fantasy. Advertisers are a canny lot and whether intuitively, or through intention, they are onto this theme. You only have to look at the titles of a recent crop of books on advertising and marketing to see the proliferation of titles that evoke the world of the magic and intuition. *Secret Formulas of the Wizard of Ads*; *The Wizard of Ads: Turning Words into Magic and Dreams*, NB (Part III of which is titled *Turning Dreams into Realities*); *Counter Intuitive Marketing: Achieve Great Results using Uncommon Sense*; *Selling Dreams: How to Make Any Product Irresistible*; and *The Dream Society: How the*

Coming Shift from Information to Imagination will Transform your Business. These titles are not academic volumes, and they are not books that analyse what the advertising industry does. These are books for people who want to be successful advertisers. Interestingly, both the *Secret Formulas of the Wizard of Ads* and its companion volume, *The Wizard of Ads*, are designed to look like a Hollywood version of a magician's book of spells. The suggestion is that advertisers themselves are partly drawn into the archetypal magic fantasy.

The advertising executive Glenn Frank observes that 'The advertising man is a liaison between the products of business and the mind of the nation'.[6] To make this liaison an effective one advertisers draw on cultural fears, desires and preoccupations. They are mythmakers and the stories they create have two primary functions. First, like ancient myths, they serve to provide a consensual framework for the society: a shared system of beliefs that make sense of the world. Secondly, and unlike ancient myths, they give the illusion that the personal lives of each and every consumer can be enriched if they take part in the magical process, not as a society but as individuals. The purpose of the advertisement is to create a 'mini-myth' that offers the opportunity for personal transformation. As Jenson notes:

> The story scenario. The customer buys feelings, experiences, and stories. This is the post-materialistic consumer demanding a story to go with the product. Food that is of good quality, tasty, and nutritious will no longer be sufficient. It must appeal to the emotions with a built-in story of status and belonging, adventure, and life style. *The packaging challenge*; The can with a story to tell – what does it look like?[7]

Some marketeers go even further. Longinotti-Buitoni, past president and CEO of Ferrari, North America, had an explicitly psychological approach in which he appropriated the tools of depth psychology, dream analysis and fidelity to emotional experience to promote products. He implored advertisers to 'Interpret the spirit of the time in order to understand which dreams will capture the customer'.[8] Later in his book, he suggests that advertisers should 'create products and services designed and engineered to convey intense emotions'.[9] Still later he observes that 'Dreams in their most common meaning, refer to an ideal, an aspiration, or a state of mind in which the proper perception of reality is rearranged'.[10] While it is quite possible to take issue about his specific interpretations of technical terminology (are dreams really a state in which the *proper* perception of reality has been rearranged?), what remains of crucial importance is his promotion of the use of psychological techniques as a means through which to manipulate the customer and, in a direct reversal of the principals of analysis, the intention that the customer should be unaware of what is happening to them. This fits neatly with Williamson's observation that the exchange of goods and services for money should appear to be ideologically neutral.

Longinotti-Buitoni goes on to propose what he terms the 'dreamketing' model. This part of his argument could almost have been culled from a Jungian textbook, albeit not a good one, and is an openly cynical attempt to deploy the resources of the advertiser in propagating a series of cultural fantasies.

Link motivations behind purchasing decisions to three fundamental dreams that fuel this business. *The dream of social recognition* (mythologically, you might say, the Adonis/Venus dream)...*The dream of freedom*. Our ultimate dream is immortality, which explains man's fascination with gods (immortal humans) or semigods, be they living on Mount Olympus or up in the Hollywood Hills...*The dream of heroism* (the Herculean dream) combines the above two dreams.[11]

As mentioned above, it is almost as though the advertiser or marketer is given the magical ability to read minds, and the right to manipulate the behaviour of others by plugging directly into powerful cultural fantasies. In what now looks like a prescient observation, Raymond Williams was onto this theme when, in 1980, he commented:

> It must not be assumed that magicians – in the case, advertising agents – disbelieve their own magic. They may have a limited professional cynicism about it, from knowing how some of the tricks are done. But fundamentally they are involved, with the rest of society, in the confusion to which the magical gestures are a response. Magic is always an unsuccessful attempt to provide meanings and values, but it is often very difficult to distinguish magic from genuine knowledge and from art.[12]

In summary, advertising promotes the belief that it is operating in an ideologically neutral manner, but this conceals the true nature of the production processes. Images of magic are used to shore up this belief and ensure the complicity of advertisers in the process. The use of archetypal motifs by advertisers is something that they do not want consumers to become aware of; indeed, they may not always recognize the extent to which they are drawing on archetypal material themselves. It is my contention that using the techniques of analytical psychology has a role to play in exposing the unconscious themes that run throughout advertisements. Importantly, this type of psychological analysis is not ideologically neutral as it aims to identify the unconscious aspects that are behind both our activities as consumers and the intentions of the 'mini myth' makers; it aims to make us more conscious and more engaged with the world in which we live.

What is Alchemy?

But what has this to do with alchemy? What is alchemy anyway, and why should it be of interest? (The story of Narcissus and his role in this process will be discussed later.) A common view of alchemy is that it was an Elizabethan practice whereby rogues and scoundrels duped unsuspecting patrons into subsidizing a flamboyant lifestyle. There is little doubt that in the heyday of alchemy, in the fifteenth and sixteenth centuries, it had its fair share of charlatans and con men. Such characters are entertainingly satirized in Ben Jonson's Jacobean play, *The Alchemist*, in its reference to the activities of the historical figure of Edward Kelly *alias* Talbot. An Oxford dropout, fraudulent lawyer, forger and exhumer of corpses, Kelly was an out and out rogue. However, alongside these tricksters other alchemists were genuine in their intentions and their aims were twofold. Their first hope was to produce gold, but their second desire was to effect an inner transformation of the psyche. Indeed, for the alchemists these two processes were bound together. As John Holmyard observes in his lucid account of the historical development of alchemy:

The Great Work of alchemy was intimately bound up with the whole religious and philosophical background, and for many who practised it the transmutation of metals was symbolical of the transmutation of imperfect man into a state of perfection. Conversely, metallic transmutation could be brought about only by divine aid and by men of pure life. These two tenets reacted upon one another and are complexly interwoven in alchemical thought.[13]

Perhaps it is less well known that as a practice alchemy is both ancient and widespread. The antecedents of Hermetic alchemy can be found in the work of Greek, Islamic and Chinese alchemists. According to Holmyard:

It appears, indeed, that one of the earliest historical mentions of alchemy is to be found in a Chinese imperial edict issued in 144 B.C., which enacted that coiners and those who made counterfeit gold should be punished by public execution. A commentator on this edict, writing about A.D. 180, explains that the Emperor Wen (about 175 B.C.) had allowed such practices, and much alchemistic gold had been made; however alchemistic gold is not really gold, and the alchemists thus lose their time and money and are left with nothing more than empty boasts.[14]

It was the alchemist's search to produce something that in actuality could never exist (a substance that transforms other metals to gold) that led Jung to see the process as fundamentally symbolic, not pseudo-scientific. As a creative language, the imagery used by alchemists belongs to the real world even although it is used to describe inner psychological events. It has to be said that to the lay reader the symbolic language of alchemical texts is pretty impenetrable. Take the following passage, which was originally published in Latin in Frankfurt in 1678, from *The Hermetic Museum* prepared by Arthur Waite for publication in English in 1898. The extract has been picked almost at random from the vast ocean of alchemical literature to illustrate the somewhat obscure nature of these texts.

The common spirit of salt, which is extracted according to the direction given in my last declaration, if there by added to it a small quality of the 'spirit of the dragon,' dissolves, volatilises, and raises together with itself in the alembic, gold and silver; just as the 'eagle,' together with the spirit of the dragon (which is found in stony places), before the spirit is separated from its body, is much more powerful in producing fixation than volatility.[15]

With practice, and a bit of specialist knowledge, it is possible to work out something of the chemical process that is being suggested. Spirit generally refers to distillation or sublimation; the dragon was an alloy of copper and silver made by warming the two together with mercury (the eagle) and so on. Although such effort does not reveal much, if anything, that would be of interest to a chemist, Jung found in this symbolic language a parallel to his own work on psychological development and transformation. He noticed in the dreams and paintings of his patients alchemical imagery, something of which his patients where almost certainly unaware. As Casement describes, here the alchemists' search for the stone that will turn base metal into gold comes to mirror the psychological work of individuation:

For him [Jung], the alchemical goal of extracting gold from base metals is mirrored in the analytical work in the gradual extraction of the unconscious gold from the base metal of consciousness to lead to the higher union of the two...What particularly excited Jung was the affinity he felt between his ideas and those in alchemy to do with archetypal transformation.[16]

Jung's fascination with the subject results in three volumes of his collected works being devoted to the subject of alchemy (*Psychology and Alchemy*, *Alchemical Studies* and *Mysterium Coniunctionis*). In them he explores the parallel between the processes of alchemy and his own emerging views on psychological development. This is a complex process as different alchemists, and different alchemical traditions, present the stages of alchemical transformation in a variety of ways. This said, underlying them all is a basic process in which the material is selected, prepared and then transformed into the philosopher's stone which can then be used to transform the base metals into gold. For Jung, the *prima material* of the alchemists is equivalent to the raw material of the as yet not individuated or untransformed psyche: the subsequent alchemical process symbolizes various aspects of individuation. The *Vas* of the alchemists, the alchemical vessel in which the transformations take place, is analogous to the analytical relationship, and also to the psyche which as a container for the alchemic changes the psyche will undergo. The *Lapis*, or the 'philosopher's stone' as it sometimes referred to, is a symbol of individuation. The *Hierosgamos*, or sacred marriage, symbolically links the ethereal and the corporeal that respectively are the outer and inner worlds of the psyche.

In chapter 5 of *Psychology and Alchemy* Jung goes further and draws parallels between the figure of Christ (as a symbol of the Self) and the lapis. Despite the seemingly controversial nature of this exercise this is a strand, albeit a slender one, that runs throughout Christian imagery. For example, take the following from the hymn *Teach me my God and King* by the metaphysical poet George Herbert (1593–1633), which is still sung today. The last verse contains the following:

> This is the famous stone
> That turneth all to gold
> For that which God doth touch and own
> Cannot for less be told.[17]

The meaning of this is not entirely obvious (like much of the hymn and, indeed, like much of alchemy). To what does the 'this' of the first line refer? Is it God's grace, or Christ, or is Herbert making some other theological statement? Whatever the precise meaning of the verse, the allusion to the symbolism of the alchemy is obvious.

To summarize, for the purposes of this chapter, it is enough to note that alchemical imagery is concerned with transformation, and that its language describes a physical change that symbolically refers to an inner change in the psyche. Such changes are part of the psyche's overall drive towards wholeness and integration. This is important because contemporary television advertising draws on this imagery to suggest the potent power of products in facilitating personal growth, enhancement and ultimately happiness. As an unconscious process, advertising is effective in drawing the culture into the arena of archetypal influence; put another way, advertisements offer the promise of self-improvement yet by the very imagery they use, and the nature of their enterprise, they cannot deliver this. To paraphrase Raymond Williams, it is the triumph of advertising that it perpetuates the 'narcissistic ideal' despite the criticism inexorably made of it by experience.[18]

Interestingly, in alchemic symbolism animals have an import role. For example, toads refer to the unpromising outer exterior of the *prima material* and our misplaced tendency to make judgements that are based on outward appearances. The raven and crow, because of their colour, symbolize a part of the alchemical process known as the *nigrego*, while swans and doves represent spirit. This type of symbolism is singled out by Jung and classified as theriomorphic symbolism; it goes beyond straightforward anthropomorphism as the animal is invested with qualities that consciousness does not normally associate with the creature. Now it seems like quite a jump from such imagery, drawing as it does on the rich veins of cultural mythology, to animals in advertising such as the dancing Anchor Butter cows or the curious Toilet Duck. But perhaps it is even stranger that we take for granted rubber ducks that dance in the shower (Imperial Leather Shower Gel), bears that have skills in martial arts (John West Salmon), bees that have hay fever (Weetabix) and cats that dance (Bacardi Breezer). What is happening here and why might it help to make products desirable?

It is certain that in a world as commercially astute as advertising the use of animals to sell products is not just a matter of whimsy. Whatever the justifications used in the meetings of the advertising agencies, animals connect with a basic or archetypal part of ourselves. It was for this reason that alchemists used animals to straddle the divide between the physical and the spiritual – or, put another way, between the conscious and the unconscious. That animals are subject to anthropomorphic treatment suggests their suitability as recipients of unconscious projections. Further, the suspicion that animals carry within themselves a vestige of part of ourselves that we have evolved away from serves to fuel archetypal fantasies. These myths and archetypal drives are tapped into by advertisers in order to suggest that their products can reconnect us to such primal aspects of our existence, are part of us that we have forgotten. Kellog's Cornflakes have an advert in which a bear in pyjamas comes downstairs, 'after hibernation' and on eating his cornflakes he magically morphs into a human. The imagery associated with the product positions it in such a way as to straddle the binary divide between the conscious and the unconscious, between our animal primeval selves and our actual existence as consumers in the early twenty-first century.

Of course, it is the case that television advertisements are full of what are colloquially referred to under the heading of special effects. However, the increasing prevalence of digital technology makes the term increasingly difficult to define, as many effects that previously required complicated optical and chemical procedures during post-production can now be created with relative ease in a digital editing and effects facility. Nonetheless, in the language of the television and film industries, special effects fall into one of two categories: visible or invisible. Invisible effects, as their name suggests, are supposed to go unnoticed. They are used to increase the naturalism of the scene. A background might be enhanced, colours enriched, skies darkened and so on. Of more interest here are the effects that draw attention to themselves: the effects that are more obviously 'magical'. In part, these have been touched on in the preceding section (talking animals, for example). But there are a couple of other ways that special effects are used. One involves the manipulation of nature to create fantastical images. For example, the Listerine tooth fairies who are unable to break past the hard enamel of the tooth to cause decay, or the erupting volcano that threatens to overtake the drivers of Fiat's Punto.

The other type of special effect involves using computer-generated visuals in similar manner to audio stings, short chords or bursts of music or sound that are used to give a particular emphasis to an image or audio-visual sequence. These 'visual-stings' help to coat advertisements with an overtly magical patina. For example, the green fumes that are given off by a shoe that is in desperate need of the help that Odor-Eaters can provide, or the whoosh of a supernatural light across some hair that changes its colour in an instant from grey to brunette. The use of this technique is widespread, and generally serves to imbue the product with supernatural qualities.

The Psychological Approach – Advertising and Narcissism
It is the contention of this chapter that advertising uses a series of mythological and magical motifs to stimulate and spur consumers into life. Sometimes advertisers appear to deploy such imagery in a knowing manner, at other times it seems more intuitive. In either case the consumer is not supposed to reflect on the imagery. Instead the hope is that it should wash over them, it should appear natural, believable and desirable.

The myth of Narcissus, in outline at least, is well known although its details are perhaps less familiar. The oldest version of the story can be found in Ovid's *Metamorphoses*.[19] Ovid tells the story in what amounts to just a few pages. Others have been less frugal in their reworking of the myth and it is a testament to the power of the original that it continues to be reworked, or to use the modern parlance 're-invented', today.[20] In summary Ovid's account is as follows.

The river nymph, Liriope, who was raped by Cephisus, gives birth to Narcissus. Liriope goes to visits Teresias, who Juno has struck blind. By way of compensation Jupiter gave him the power to foretell the future and he tells Liriope that Narcissus will have a long life, providing that 'He does not come to know himself'. Aged 16 and still a virgin ('his young soft body housed a pride so unyielding that none of those boys or girls dared to touch him') the nymph Echo sees him from her hiding place in the woods and instantly falls in love with him. She emerges and throws her arms around Narcissus. He responds, 'Away with these embraces! I would die before I would have you touch me!' Echo's ability to converse is limited to repeating the words of others and she responds, 'I would have you touch me!' Echo's beauty fades and she wastes away until only her voice is left, the part of her that lives on today. One of Narcissus' spurned lovers prays, 'May he himself fall in love with another, as we have done with him! May he too be unable to gain his loved one!' The plea is granted by Nemesis. Narcissus comes across a clear pool and while taking a drink falls in love with the beautiful reflection that he sees. 'Unwittingly, he desired himself, and was the object of his own approval.' Eventually he realizes that 'Alas! I am the boy I see...I am on fire with love for my own self'. With this recognition his beauty fades and 'Nothing remained of the body that Echo had once loved'. In its place is 'a flower with a circle of white petals around a yellow centre'. Echo sees what happens and grieves for Narcissus. But even when taken into the underworld Narcissus continues to gaze at himself in the river Styx.

The richness of this mythological imagery facilitates the process of projection and identification and it is, therefore, unsurprising that it finds its way into many television advertisements. In ideological terms it passes off culture for nature – it hegemonizes the myth of transformation and perfection and re-presents it in microcosm as an opportunity for the individual. For example, the advertisement for Organics with essential oils shows a woman gazing at her reflection in every reflective surface she encounters, while Clairol's Natural Tones claims that your newly dyed hair will have 'A beauty all your own'. This is a process of projection in which internal narcissistic unconscious desires are transferred onto objects in the outer world: a process whose roots lie in a deep-seated need for a clear sense of self-identity, or, to use a more Jungian terminology, individuation.

Jung's writings about narcissism are less extensive than Freud's. Jung also took a rather different view as he regarded activities that are typically thought of as narcissistic as being part of a normal healthy psychological life. Our task, like that faced by Narcissus, is to understand the difference between our self and the idealized image of ourselves that is reflected in the world. In essence the challenge is to find our identity. In contemporary society the multiplicity of self-images gives unprecedented opportunities to play fast and free – to loosen our identities to play and explore. But in this respect what advertising offers is more meretricious than meritorious, for the identities offer only an ephemeral level of satisfaction. Coming to recognize this and engaging with life in a playful, but conscious, manner, is part of growing up. This involves accepting that in our commodity-driven, consumerist and materialist culture, goods have a role to play in the formation our own identities. As the Jungian analyst Jacoby puts it:

> All this seems to indicate that the intense preoccupation of many young people with themselves is an important part of the process of finding their own identity, an appropriate aspect of this phase of development – it is, in other words, caused by Nemesis (or Fate).[21]

Jung also thought that under certain circumstances narcissism could become pathological, although he thought this relatively rare. More typically, Jung regarded narcissistic development as a lifelong task that was closely related to the process of individuation. This is consistent with the post-Jungian position where there are some useful points of contact with psychoanalytic theory. This is particularly the case with the work of Heinz Kohut who suggests that narcissism starts in infancy.[22] In the scenario outlined by Kohut, the baby 'mirrors' the mother who encourages the baby's exhibitionism and the sense that the baby is indeed the centre of the world. Gradually the loving mother introduces the child to reality and in so doing illusions are replaced with a more grounded perspective. This marks a move away from illusion and exhibitionism and what emerges is a strong sense of self and a defined set of achievements. This happens somewhere between two and four years of age. Because of the need to find a source of goodness that is greater than itself, at the same time, the mother is idealized as a projection of the baby's own inflated sense of its own goodness. In time (between four and six years) this is also transformed, but this time the change is into ideals and values. In some senses this strays away from the Jungian position which argues that the self is something that is forged out of the parent/child bond and not something that is archetypal, or innate. However, it is not a marked shift to suggest that actually the role of the parent is to provide an external source for the projection of the baby's archetypal fantasies that are gradually dissolved, and in so doing a healthy psychological regime is established. Indeed, this seems to mirror, rather nicely, the analytical situation where the analyst is the object of transference fantasies and works with the analysand as they become aware of this process. Further as Andrew Samuels notes:

> Transmuting internalisations, through the working out of self-object [external person or thing] transferences in analysis (mirroring or idealising) can repair damage done to the nuclear self by parental psychopathology, environmental defect or a poor fit between infant and mother.[23]

In part, the imagery of advertising plays on this need to 'repair damage done to the nuclear self' by offering the potential for self-improvement through the consumption of images and the purchasing of products. The potency of this need can be seen in the direct association that exists between narcissistic behaviour and the activities of consumers. The following profile has been extracted from Nathan Schwartz-Salant's work *Narcissism and Character Transformation*.[24] The most relevant elements have been selected from the comprehensive profile that Schwartz-Salant creates of narcissistic qualities and behaviours. Importantly he notes that a narcissistic character '*Lacks penetrability*:... whatever one says is immediately transformed by that person into a story or fantasy or idea about himself (or herself)'.[25] Of course, this is an ideal state for advertisers, as has already been identified one of the self-confessed goals of advertising is to persuade potential customers to buy into a myth, or supposed need in themselves.

Schwartz-Salant goes on to note that the narcissistic person '*Cannot tolerate criticism*:... the person with a narcissistic character disorder has so little sense of identity...that any criticism at all is seen as personal threat'.[26] Consequently, advertisers tend to stay away from strategies that suggest the consumer is in some way inadequate. It is much better to suggest how they might have even better lives. As the advert for Lenor's Natural Balance puts it, 'where can you feel refreshed?'. Interestingly, some advertisements go as far as parodying themselves, as in the ice cream advert which sends up the search for self-enlightenment in a mock documentary of people who claim to have found their inner-selves by eating Häagen-Dazs ice cream. Schwartz-Salant also notes that the narcissist '*Cannot integrate a synthetic approach*:....the narcissistic character is pre-symbolic, unable to appreciate the reality of the symbol...symbolic reality will not exist for the narcissistic character'.[27] Again, this is useful for advertisers who do not necessarily want customers to be engaged in a conscious fashion with the symbolic realm.

Interestingly, typically narcissistic behaviour often takes pride in having no needs, 'while doing a great deal for others. "I can do it" is often their motto'.[28] This attribute is played on by many advertisements targeted, particularly, at housewives. The suggestion satisfaction can be achieved by doing more for your family, is a powerful one even if it is at expense of not taking care of yourself. Some adverts go so far as to suggest that you might displace the father's role in the family by food. For example, the McCain's advert for oven-ready chips in which a little girl ponders whether she prefers 'Daddy or Chips?' (The question is repeated in a mantra like manner throughout much of the advert.) The outcome is never really in any doubt, and Dad comes a clear second behind the chips. The humour of the advert masks what actually amounts to something of a power struggle within the family unit. Significantly, the question is not whether the daughter prefers Mummy or Chips. The mother's role as provider is secure, it is the absent father who is at risk: an attitude of mind that the advert encourages. The desire for chips, for what the child wants, displaces the need for a father.

Echoing some of the observations of Raymond Williams, it is significant that narcissistic behaviour is characterized by a lack of sense of history or process, 'Situations are not really *experienced* because every situation is met out of the ego's complex of self-esteem'.[29] The narcissistic character also demonstrates, *'Disturbed masculine and feminine functioning:...* for men the *anima* problem is usually central, while for women the problem is mainly with the *animus'*.[30] Schwartz-Salant also notes until the potential for positive archetypal constellation is activated the within the narcissistic person that '...reflection and imagination are superficial; flashiness substitutes for depth'.[31] Again this is deployed by advertisers in suggesting that a 'high-gloss' lifestyle will triumph over the more mundane experience of everyday life. In this sense, the television screen is like the pool into which Narcissus gazed. Advertisers encourage us to fall in love with ourselves, and to aspire to be as beautiful and self-absorbed as Narcissus.

To conclude, in bringing together the themes of alchemy and narcissism in a psychological exploration of television advertising the intention was to tease out some of the psychological reasons behind the appeal and effectiveness of television advertisements. While adverts purport to offer great opportunities to transform our lives, in reality they pander to narcissistic tendencies. The idealized self-image is, of course, both unattainable and undesirable as the natural trajectory of psychological growth is towards wholeness and *not* perfection. Jacoby sums up as follows:

> Jung also describes precisely those traits and symptoms most evident in the therapeutic analysis of individuals with narcissistic problems: possessiveness, the drive for prestige, discontentedness, the sense of being hemmed in, envy, and jealousy. Such analysands generally find it impossible for a long time to really accept that 'I am only that'; any limitation of their unconscious claims to perfection implies

to them that others regard them as totally worthless, and they then view themselves accordingly.[32]

The list almost serves as a paradigm of consumer behaviours: possessiveness, the drive for prestige, discontentedness. These are attitudes that are stimulated in consumers by advertisements with the clear suggestion that the purchase of a product will remedy the problem; in fact, it can do the opposite. But to end on a more optimistic note perhaps it should not be forgotten that the psyche has an innate tendency to heal itself. Maybe the current fascination with self-improvement is actually the psyche's way of telling us to move on although the problem is so large that even our stubborn consciousnesses have to recognize what is happening. Jacoby puts it like this:

It seems to me, then, that our myth deals with the human drive for self-knowledge and self-realization, with the admonition 'Become who you are!' – and thus is implies the possibility of transcending the narrower forms of narcissistic problems.

Notes

1. Williamson, J. *Decoding Advertisements: Ideology and Meaning in Advertising.* (Marion Boyers: London, 1978), p. 141. Emphasis as original.
2. *Ibid.*, p. 140.
3. *Ibid.*, p. 140.
4. *Ibid.*, p. 141.
5. Williams, R. 'Advertising: the Magic System' in *Problems in Materialism and Culture.* (Verso: London, 1980), p. 185. (Emphasis as original.)
6. Glenn Frank, quoted in Williams, R., *The Wizard of Ads: Turning Words into Magic and Dreams.* (Bard Press, Austin Texas, 1998), p. 21.
7. Jenson, R. *The Dream Society: How the Coming Shift from Information to Imagination will Transform your Business.* (McGraw-Hill: New York, 1999), p. 29. Emphasis as original.
8. Longinotti-Buitoni, L. G. with Longinotti-Buitoni, K. *Selling Dreams: How to Make Any Product Irresistible.* (Simon and Schuster: New York, 1999), p. 15.
9. *Ibid.*, p. 15.
10. *Ibid.*, p. 23.
11. *Ibid.*, pp. 76–77.
12. Williams, R. 'Advertising: the Magic System' in *Problems in Materialism and Culture.* (Verso: London, 1980), p. 189.
13. Holmyard, J. *Alchemy.* (Penguin Books: Harmondsworth, 1957), p. 152.
14. *Ibid.*, p. 31.
15. Valentius, B. 'The Practica, with Twelve Keys, and an Appendix Thereto, Concerning the Great Stone of the Ancient Sages'. In, *The Hermetic Museum* (eds) Waite, A. (London, 1893), p. 355.
16. Casement, A. *Carl Gustav Jung.* (Sage: London, 2001), pp. 53–54.
17. Herbert, G. *Teach me my God and King,* source Hymns and Psalms: A Methodist and Ecumenical Hymn Book. (The Methodist Publishing House: London, 1983). Hymn number 803.

18. Williams, R. 'Advertising: the Magic System' in *Problems in Materialism and Culture*. (Verso: London, 1980), p. 188.

19. Ovid, *The Metamorphoses of Ovid*. Trans, Innes, M. M. (Penguin: Harmondsworth, 1955). pp. 83–87.

20. Cf. Vinge, L. *The Narcissus Theme in Western Literature up to the Early Nineteenth Century*. Trans., R. Dewsnap (Gleerups: Lund, 1967).

21. Jacoby, M. *Individuation and Narcissism: The Psychology of Self in Jung and Kohut*. (Routledge: London, 1990), p. 27.

22. Kohut, H., *The Analysis of Self*. (International Universities Press: New York: 1971) c.f. and Kohut, H. *The Restoration of Self*. (International Universities Press: New York: 1977).

23. Samuels, A. *Jung and the Post-Jungians*. (Routledge: London, 1985), p. 125.

24. Extracted from: Schwartz-Salant, N. *Narcissism and Character Transformation: The Psychology of Narcissistic Character Disorders*. (Inner City Books: Toronto, 1982), pp. 37–41.

25. *Ibid.*, pp. 37–38.

26. *Ibid.*, p. 38.

27. *Ibid.*, p. 38.

28. *Ibid.*, p. 39.

29. *Ibid.*, p. 39.

30. *Ibid.*, p. 40.

31. *Ibid.*, p. 41.

32. Jacoby, M. *Individuation and Narcissism: The Psychology of Self in Jung and Kohut*. (Routledge: London, 1990), pp. 25–26.

33. Jacoby, M. *Individuation and Narcissism: The Psychology of Self in Jung and Kohut*. (Routledge: London, 1990), p. 29.

6

Star Trek: Some Jungian Thoughts

The original *Star Trek* series is now four decades old. The year 1966 saw the 'big bang' of the *Star Trek* universe, a phenomenon that has continued to expand at an exponential rate to the extent that it currently includes: four television series *Star Trek*, (54 episodes), *Star Trek: The Next Generation*, (*TNG*, 178 episodes), *Star Trek*: *Deep Space Nine*, (*DS9*, 174 episodes, *Star Trek: Voyager*, (169 episodes), *Enterprise* (98, episodes), movies (ten, with an eleventh due in 2008), 130 novels, a cartoon series, over 500 fan publications, countless toys, numerous other spin-offs – some official, some not.

Given this remarkable success it is perhaps unsurprising that books have sprung up which chart the history and development of each of the series. *The Star Trek Encyclopaedia: a Reference Guide to the Future* records in meticulous detail every aspect of the fictional world of *Star Trek*. (Did you know that an inverse tachyon beam is used to study temporal phenomena?) Without doubt, it is essential reading for all die-hard fans. Perhaps more surprising are the books that deal in a no less serious manner with topics such as the metaphysics of *Star Trek*, or the biology of *Star Trek* and the physics of *Star Trek*. (The last book even has a forward by the eminent physicist Stephen Hawkins who is also a fan and who made a guest-star appearance in the episode *Descent, Part 1*, TNG.) Still more surprising are the self-help books that are based on the series. *Make it so: Leadership Lessons from Star Trek: The Next Generation* proudly proclaims to be 'The *Business Week* and *Entrepreneur* magazine bestseller!'[1] While *Boldly Live as You've Never Lived Before*, offers a personality test in which the resulting profile rates your abilities as: Leader (Kirk, Picard, Sisko Janeway); Warrior (Worf, Kira, B'Elanna, Scotty[!]); Analyst (Spock, Dax, Data, Q, Odo, Tuvok); and Relator (Guinan, Troi, McCoy, Bashir, Kes). Subsequent sections of the book explain how to improve your scores and which episodes of *Star Trek* to watch in preparation for your inner work.

It is tempting to dismiss both the fanatical obsession with detail in the encyclopaedia and the somewhat literal application of *Star Trek*'s values and characters to everyday life. But perhaps there might be some merit in wondering why this state of affairs has come about. What is it about *Star Trek* that has managed to get inside the minds of so many people? One explanation lies in the psychological and mythological structure of the series. Far from being based around science and logic (The starship Enterprise is supposed to be a scientific vessel, albeit a well-armed one) the series actually deals with psychological themes and archetypal situations and characters. Further, the view of humanity offered by *Star Trek* is complex and dark. This is quite at odds with the normal interpretation of the series which typically regards the futuristic world of *Star Trek* as showing a utopian view of the future and offering an essentially positive view of human nature.

Cyborgs – The Challenge of Being Human in *Star Trek*

To write about cyborgs is to step into a set of postmodern debates about nature and our cultural state. This territory is effectively mapped in books such as Chris Gray's *The Cyborg Handbook* (1995) and Claudia Springer's *Electronic Eros: Bodies and Desire in the Postindustrial Age* (1996): there are many others. For the purposes of this chapter it is enough to note that cyborgs are a mixture of organic matter and machine. In this respect they are not computers, nor robots, both of which are mechanical devices. *Star Trek* has both robots and cyborgs: Data (Brent Spiner) and his evil twin brother, Lore (also Brent Spiner), are androids (a robot made to look human); the Borg, as their name suggests, are cyborgs. A further category of human simulacra is the Emergency Medical Hologram (EMH) in *Voyager* who has the distinction, amongst holographic characters, of actually becoming conscious. Despite these differences, all these characters are on a similar trajectory; what they share is a desire to become *fully* human. This is interesting as it has the effect of foregrounding in the series questions about what being human means. As already suggested, at the very root of the *Star Trek* universe is a deep ambivalence over the value that should be placed on humankind.

Cyborgs in *Star Trek* are particularly interesting in the way they blur the distinction between what is human and what is machine. Another way of putting this would be to say that in the world of *Star Trek* the dividing line between organic and non-organic is not always clear. For example, on the ship's holodeck it is possible to create from inorganic matter solid three-dimensional holograms that appear in all respects to be real. Likewise, the replicators (an essential part of life onboard any starship) can reproduce mechanical and electronic parts or even chemicals and food. Such seemingly magical behaviour points us towards the world of myth and legend and perhaps this is one of the reasons that the science-fiction genre remains appealing: it offers both a technologically sophisticated fantasy and a magical, or mythological, view of the future. From the perspective of analytical psychology it is reasonable, albeit with a little license, to claim that outer space mirrors inner space, a point that will be revisited later.

Of the numerous species that the various crews of *Star Trek* encounter it is the Borg who stands out. The species comes from the Delta Quadrant of the galaxy, many light years from Federation Space. (The Delta Quadrant also provides the setting for the *Star Trek* series Voyager.) This very distance renders them as something that is apparently far removed from humanity. The Borg with their mechanically enhanced bodies form part of a subspace network known as the Collective whose distinguishing feature is joint consciousness which is shared to the extent that it almost excludes individual existence. As will become clear, the tension between being an individual and being part of a wider collective is also part of life onboard the Enterprise. The Collective are presided over by a Queen (Alice Krige). She is the linchpin of Borg society to that extent that when she is killed onboard Enertprise-E, the Borg lose their basic command and control structure, (*Star Trek: First Contact*, TNG). As a race, the Borg are aggressive predators who survive by conquering other species and assimilating their civilizations and technologies. The Enterprise encounters the Borg at regular intervals throughout *Star Trek*. They were introduced in *The Next Generation Episode* (TNG) *Q Who* and continue to have a role to play right up to the final episode of the Voyager series, *Endgame*.

One reading of the Borg would be to see the threat that they pose as one of racial assimilation. In their pale grey skin and heavily prosthetic exteriors the distinctions between races disappears. Certainly in their quest to assimilate other races they are reminiscent of the exploits of other conquering nations. Colonialization, cultural imperialism, racism, fear of large totalizing organizations, whether political or corporate, are all evoked by their behaviour. Occasionally, episodes of *The Next Generation* explicitly address such themes such as in *I Borg* (TNG) where the Enterprise takes onboard Third of Five (Jonathan Del Arco), a Borg who is dying. During the episode, the crew hatch a plan to infect him with a virus with the intention of returning Third of Five to infect the rest of the Collective. The plan is eventually vetoed by Picard as Third of Five begins to develop a sense of self-identity and, on doing so, he is renamed Hugh (a bad pun on 'Who'). During this episode Hugh encounters Guinan (Whoopi Goldberg), one of the few members of the El-Aurian race to have survived the Borg's assimilation. As Hastie comments, this lets the episode directly address questions of race and colonialization:

> Resembling stereotypical African dress, Guinan's gowns thus help to code her story as one analogous to the 'diaspora' of Africans who were 'assimilated' and then 'regenerated' as slaves in the United States. Her people, she tells us, were scattered throughout the galaxy after the Borg came for them, and they no longer have a 'home'.[2]

At the end of the episode Hugh elects to return to the Borg, and Picard muses, 'Perhaps that's the most pernicious programme of all: the knowledge of self-being spread through the collective'. Hastie comments:

> Of course, the starship crew uncritically qualifies this pernicious act not as one of 'assimilation' (to become more like the starship), nor as one of genocide, but instead as one of 'resurrection': They are merely attempting to reconstruct (or deconstruct) the Borg back into individuals.[3]

This is interesting, because in one sense Hastie is correct and, indeed, this type of interpretation is to all intents and purposes a fairly typical media or cultural studies type of 'reading'. But another interpretation is possible. Instead of seeing the episode as a political metaphor, it is possible to interpret Picard's remarks both politically and psychologically. In so doing the act of making Hugh conscious is pernicious and potentially destructive because consciousness and self-awareness are difficult to cope with. They pose challenges to the structure and order of society as they require a strong ego-identity that can withstand contradictions caused when the unconscious and consciousness come into play. As Jung puts it, 'Everyone who becomes conscious of even a fraction of his unconscious gets outside his own time and social stratum into a kind of solitude'.[4] Elsewhere he remarks that not only is this type of tension inevitable it is actually positive and an essential part of the teleological aspects of individuation, 'Man needs difficulties; they are necessary for health'.[5]

At different points in *Star Trek* human characters are assimilated into the Borg collective, namely Picard and Seven of Nine (Jeri Ryan). The nature of their assimilations are somewhat different. As a child Seven of Nine was assimilated by the Borg and became, in a psychological sense, part of the collective. By contrast, Picard was assimilated in the episode *Best of Both Worlds, Part 1* where he became Locutus of Borg. His transformation was merely temporary and it was possible for him to return him to fully human status. The result of this is that Seven of Nine has a more ambiguous relationship with the Borg collective. She first appears in *Scorpion, Part II* where the truth about her background is gradually revealed. A quality shared by both Seven and Picard is that they straddle bridge between the human and the alien and, as such, they are anomalous characters who know the extent to which they contain the capacity for both good and evil. This gives them a mythological quality, as Barrett notes:

> So the first 'monster' explicitly poses the question of what it means to be human. In some ways 'Frankenstein' embodies a more 'human' set of values than the humans around him. He aspires to a human existence, as do the characters in *Star Trek* who have been 'created' by humans. Figures such as Data, Seven and the EMH [emergency medical hologram] are partly allegorical.[6]

But cyborg technology *per se* is not necessarily bad in the world of *Star Trek*. Picard has an artificial heart, Worf (Michael Dorn) a new backbone, Geordi Laforge (LeVar Burton) wears a visor that lets him see (although it is not always reliable). The aim of all this 'good' technology is to enhance the individual; by contrast, Borg technology removes any sense of uniqueness or individuality.

Myth and Narrative

As a series *Star Trek* has a particular fascination with time, time travel and the paradoxes that emerge. A lot of science-fiction films worry about changing the past and the effects this might have on the future. There are no such anxieties in *Star Trek*. Here the past is never fixed and the future can always be altered. Of course, it is possible to engage with *Star Trek*'s representation of time and space and try to figure out its logical and internal consistency, but it seems much easier to say that space-time in the series uses a mythological logic.[7] In so doing, it does not attempt to provide a consistent rational narrative, instead it creates a universe that is essentially magical and mythical. Science fiction is well suited to such fantasies. Indeed, in its preoccupation with time travel it is not unreasonable to claim that the genre is inherently psychological, as Jung comments:

Anything psychic is Janus faced - it looks both backwards and forwards. Because it is evolving, it is also preparing the future. Were this not so, intentions, aims, plans, calculations, predictions and premonitions would be psychological impossibilities.[8]

Perhaps the most obvious example of this type of magical, mythic transformation of space is provided by the holodeck. The holodeck permits the simulation of virtually any environment or person with degree of fidelity that renders it virtually indistinguishable from reality. At one level this is a brilliant narrative ruse. In one stroke the programme makers created a mechanism that overcomes the conflict between the restricted space of a starship, or space station and the narrative need for new characters, locations and settings. While this may have provided the motivation for the introduction of the device (the original series was without holodecks), it has the effect of foregrounding the importance of fantasy. The holodeck is somewhere the crew go to escape, to relax and to exercise. Sometimes the holodecks are used to provide a scientific testing ground for new theories where re-engineered objects and the like can be tried out before they are put to use. In the episode *Learning Curve* (Voyager) the bridge of Voyager is simulated. But the holodeck also serves as a virtual entertainment environment with simulations ranging from King Arthur's Court (*The Way of the Warrior,* Deep Space 9), Lake Como (*The Swarm,* Voyager) and a nineteenth-century town on the American wild frontier (*A Fist Full of Datas*, TNG). Effectively, this places images and fantasies centre stage in *Star Trek* and this is a very Jungian activity. As Jung comments: '...the psyche consists essentially of images... just as the material of the body that is ready for life has need of the psyche in order to be capable of life, so the psyche presupposes that living body in order that its images may live'.[9]

One of the features of the holodeck is that the crew are able to create and store personal holodeck programmes. Sometimes they do this with the most obvious of psychological intentions. For example, Captain Janeway creates a gothic romance, in which she seeks to provide a counterbalance to her overtly rationalist approach to her duties as Captain. In the episode *Blood Fever* a medical programme is created with the intention of helping Ensign Vorik (Alexander Enberg) at *Pon Farr* – the Vulcan mating season, an event which occurs every seven years in an adult Vulcan's life. What is important about these holodeck fantasies is that they are every bit as 'real' as the world outside the holodeck. This seems to fit well with Jung's definition of fantasy and the assertion that the inner world of the unconscious is as real as anything else.

The psyche creates reality every day. The only expression I can use for this activity is *fantasy*. Fantasy is just as much feeling as thinking; as much intuition as sensation. There is no psychic function that, through fantasy, is not inextricably bound up with the other psychic functions. Sometimes it appears in primordial form, sometimes it is the ultimate and boldest product of all our faculties combined. Fantasy, therefore, seems to me the clearest expression of the specific activity of the psyche. It is, pre-eminently, the creative activity from which the answers to all answerable questions come; it is the mother of all possibilities, where, like all psychological opposites, the inner and outer worlds are joined together in living union.[10]

Amidst the high-tech environment of *Star Trek* the holodeck is a curiously unreliable piece of technology. In the original series it was the transporters that were likely to malfunction with disastrous consequences. In so doing they provided one of the ways for the series to address explicitly psychological themes. In *The Enemy Within*, the transporter split Kirk into two different Captains: the civilized Kirk and the savage Kirk. The episode shows quite literally, and somewhat crudely, a coming face-to-face with the shadow. The episode is not about the Freudian construct of the id, which needs to be repressed. This representation of the shadow is made evident in showing that the 'persona' Kirk is unable to function without his shadow as he finds decision making difficult and he is unsure of himself. The message is clear, and overt, if more than a little heavy-handed – the shadow is an essential part of the psyche and it is essential that it is accepted and integrated. Fortunately the ship's engineer, Scotty, is able to reunite the two Kirks, again using the transporter. The episode is pretty self-conscious about its psychological thesis, if somewhat mechanistic in how it depicts the workings of the psyche. As Dr McCoy comments to Kirk, 'We all have a darker side; we need it; it's half of who we are; it's not really ugly, it's human'. Or, as Jung puts it:

> We carry our past with us, to wit, the primitive and inferior man with his desires and emotions, and it is only with enormous effort that we can detach ourselves from this burden. If it comes to a neurosis, we invariably have to deal with a considerably intensified shadow. And if such a person wants to be cured it is necessary to find a way in which his conscious personality and his shadow can live together.[11]

While transporter accidents do happen in *The Next Generation* (as in *Second Chances*) it is more likely to be the holodecks that misbehave. This reinforces both the narrative and psychological *need* for the holodecks. After all, why keep something on board a starship that is so much trouble? The answer is that escapism is essential for the crew. From a Jungian perspective it is not surprising that the holodeck fantasies go wrong. When dealing with unconscious material we find ourselves in potentially dangerous situations. This said, it is not so much that the unconscious itself is dangerous, it is more that faced with fantasies of the unconscious, panic can set in, because it is all too easy to lose control. Barbara Hannah puts it like this:

> It may be difficult for the unprepared reader to understand why facing the unknown in ourselves is a 'dangerous enterprise'. [*Star Trek* reference unintended] Only experience can teach one what a terrifying enterprise it is to turn away from the familiar affairs of our conscious world and face the entirely unknown in the inner, unconscious world.[12]

Jung was adamant that in dealing with the psyche it was essential to overcome the artificial split between the unconscious and consciousness. Partly this happens naturally in dreams and in moments of parapraxis (the so-called 'Freudian Slip'), where repressed material finds its way into conscious life. But Jung also suggested that a more deliberate path could be taken in which what he termed the 'transcendent function' is activated. When this happens in therapy, the analyst helps the analysand to bring consciousness and the unconscious together. As Casement observes:

The synthetic approach, [which activates the transcendent function] according to Jung, is one that values symbolic meaning in dream images or fantasies in their own right rather than reducing them to being caused by something in the individual's childhood. In this way, unconscious phenomena are regarded as if they had intention and purpose (teleology) pointing to future psychological development.[13]

This is just how the holodeck functions in *Star Trek* narratives. In some episodes characters in the holodeck come to life and try to persuade the crew that the holodeck fantasy is real. In psychological terms, this can be reconceptualized as the unconscious invading consciousness to such an extent that it becomes quite impossible to relate to the physical world in a meaningful manner. Take *Ship in a Bottle* (TNG), Moriarty (Daniel Davis) recreates the Enterprise in its entirety on a holodeck, so even when the crew think they have left the holodeck they are, in fact, still in it. Equally intriguing is the episode *11001001*. Here, Minuet (Carolyn McCormick) plays a character in a holographic simulation of a New Orleans jazz club. However, Minuet is 'an enhanced programme' designed to respond specifically to Riker's expectations. If the transporter incidents explore the shadow, then this holodeck programme explores the *anima*, a theme which is repeated in *Booby Trap* (TNG) where Geordi, the ship's Chief Engineer, falls in love with a holodeck illusion. In this case it is Dr Leah Brahms (Susan Gibney) who was responsible for much of the design of the warp engines on Enterprise-D. Perhaps it is not surprising that when Geordi eventually does meet the real Leah they do not get along. She is highly critical of his modifications to her designs and not at all happy about being replicated on a holodeck without her permission. This plays out very neatly what Jung has described as the two faces of the *anima*.[14]

No man is so entirely masculine that he has nothing feminine in him. The fact is, rather, that very masculine men have – carefully guarded and hidden - a very soft emotional life, often incorrectly described as 'feminine'. A man counts it a virtue to repress his feminine traits as much as possible, just as woman, at least until recently, considered it unbecoming to be 'mannish'. The repression of feminine traits and inclinations naturally causes these contrasexual demands to accumulate in the unconscious.[15]

In *Hollow Pursuits* (TNG) Reginald Barclay finds he is at his psychological best in the holodeck. Although he suffers from what in *Star Trek* terminology is referred to as 'Holodiction', it is precisely the experiences he has in these imaginary worlds that equip him to deal with daily life on board the Enterprise. The episode is unusual on several accounts not least because in Barclay's holodeck fantasy Deanna Troi (Marina Sirtis) (the ship's counsellor) and Beverly Crusher (Gates McFadden – the doctor on the Enterprise) stand around in various states of undress and sexual readiness. You might have thought that given the quasi-military nature of life in Starfleet that Barclay would find himself in serious trouble. But far from it, in fact, in contrast to Leah, Troi regards her virtual body as something that is quite separate to her actual body. Instead, as the ship's counsellor she begins to teach Barclay how to make friends, relate to the crew and how to develop his self-confidence. Sarah Projansky notes in *When the Body Speaks:*

Given the parallels between the diegetic holodeck and the television text in terms of representation, when Troi and the narrative absolve Barclay of guilt for looking at women without their consent they also absolve the spectator of any responsibility for objectifying women's [virtual] bodies...[16]

While not wanting to gainsay or play down Projansky's very real concerns about legitimating voyeuristic activity, it is perhaps not so surprising that Barclay, who found it difficult to relate to any of his crewmates, was engaging in sexual fantasies. His unconscious released a complementary opposite: what cannot be coped with in the conscious world, finds expression in the unconscious. Projansky confuses an archetypal fantasy with the real world – Barclay's fantasies refer to inner figures, not real people. What this episode shows is the attraction of the unconscious and its strong erotic component as unconscious material can have a strong sexual charge. Instead of being judgemental about Barclay's fantasies, Troi adopts a quasi-Jungian attitude; she accepts his fantasies and uses them as a starting point for Barclay to engage with the real world in a more meaningful, productive and related fashion.

Psychological Themes in *Star Trek*

As Thomas Richards has pointed out in *The Meaning of Star Trek*, most of the characters in *The Next Generation* come from unstable family backgrounds. Picard went against his father's wishes by entering the Starfleet Academy and was then disowned. Riker's mother died when he was two and his father, Kyle Riker (Mitchell Ryan), abandoned him aged fifteen, he was estranged from his father until a reunion some 30 years later aboard the Enterprise-D. Worf's (Michael Dorn) parents were killed in the Khitomer massacre, raised as an adopted child on earth by a Russian couple, Sergey Rozhenko (Thodore Bikel) and Helena Rozhenko (Georgia Brown). Dr Crusher (Gates McFadden) is a widow and single mother and so on. Perhaps this is one of the reasons the series is concerned with the individual's search for satisfying relationships, something that the crew of the Enterprise in *The Next Generation* are not particularly successful at. Relationships on board, when they happen at all, tend to be unstable – much like the holodecks and transporters. Virtually no mention is made of families and children or births are rare – something that can be attributed to the apparent lack of sexual activity on starships, at least in the earlier series, (*Deep Space 9* is a different matter). All this indicates the manner in which the series place a particular value on the notion of the individual. It follows that one of the greatest threats posed to characters in *Star Trek* is that the individual will 'break down' and that a sense of self-identity will be lost. As Richards observes,

Threats to identity in *Star Trek* never come from within the characters themselves. No character is ever in danger of losing his mind for internal, psychological reasons. Threat to the integrity of the personality always turns out to come from the outside.[17]

While this is certainly along the right lines it is also a somewhat literal interpretation of events. By way of an alternative, perhaps in the 'other' we find a broken off part of the psyche: a part of the personality that has yet to come into consciousness and which is projected onto the outside world. Put another way, an interpretation from the perspective of depth psychology involves getting inside the material and viewing it not in concrete materialist terms but rather from the perspective of the psyche – in terms of image and metaphor. It is important to stress that this does not mean that political, ideological, social and cultural factors are ignored. In reality quite the opposite is suggested by this approach. What it does mean is that these elements are re-framed and seen in a psychological light. Such a re-framing of the events in our lives is integral to the process of individuation. As Jung puts it:

> Individualism means deliberately stressing and giving prominence to some supposed peculiarity, rather than to collective considerations and obligations. But individuation means precisely the better and more complete fulfilment of the collective qualities of the human being, since adequate consideration of the peculiarity of the individual is more conducive to better social achievement then when the peculiarity is neglected or suppressed.[18]

A good example of this is the distinctive, and unusually bleak, episode *Chain of Command, Part 2*, (TNG) in which Picard is graphically tortured by the Cardassian Gul Madred (David Warner). As part of his interrogation Picard is injected with a truth drug

Picard (Patrick Stewart) is Tortured in *Chain of Command*

which means he has no option but to answer the questions put to him by Madred. The remainder of the episode concerns the sadistic torture of Picard during which he is implanted with a mechanical device in his chest whose sole purpose is to inflict pain. Madred's technique is to ask Picard how many lights he can see. There are four lights, and Picard tells him so. Madred suggests that there are five and activates the device. Picard continues to tell the truth despite its painful consequences. Making the episode even more disturbing, Madred is portrayed as a cultured and sophisticated Cardassian. One of the most distressing scenes occurs when Madred brings his daughter to watch Picard's interrogation. The contrast between a father casually spending time with his daughter and the agony of Picard is acute and disturbing.

The episode is a complex one and operates on a number of levels. Partly it acts as a commentary on the ability of civilized people to carry out barbaric acts. As Jung observes, 'The dammed-up instinctual forces in civilised man are immensely destructive'.[19] The suggestion is that the more that the unconscious is repressed and smothered by a patina of civilized life, the more it grows in strength so that when it does eventually make its presence felt it does so in a particularly violent and destructive manner. Jung, therefore, suggests that the best course of action is to pay attention to the unconscious and to become aware of its role.

> The inner voice...makes us conscious of the evil from which the whole community is suffering, whether it be the nation or the whole human race. But it presents this evil in an individual form, so that one might at first suppose it to be only and individual characteristic.[20]

This is precisely what happens in *Chain of Command* as Madred's pleasure in the torture of Picard comes to stand for the values of Cardassian culture in general. Here, as throughout *Star Trek*, 'evil' (or some Jungians might say the shadow) is always located in the 'other'. The numerous races that populate the outer space of *Star Trek* mirror the diversity of races and cultures on earth. But it is worlds outside the United Federation of Planets which pose a direct threat to the 'stability' of this sector of space. The work of the Federation in initiating what in *Star Trek* terminology is referred to as 'First Contact' and the Federation's aggressive defence capabilities are dangerously close to legitimating the colonial and conquering actions of powerful nations in the contemporary world. While retaining these observations it is also possible to interpret them in a more psychological light. To do so reveals the extent to which we have become disassociated from our psyche. It also demonstrates how imperative it is for Picard to maintain his grasp of reality – there a no circumstances under which he is prepared to say that there are five lights. Jung comments:

> The encounter with the dark half of the personality, or 'shadow', comes about of its own accord in any moderately thorough treatment...I have often been asked, 'And what do you *do* about it?' I do nothing...Not that I am passive or inactive meanwhile: I help the patient to understand all the things that the unconscious produces during the conflict...Nor is the patient inactive; he must do the right thing, and do it with all his might, in order to prevent the pressure of evil from becoming too powerful in him.[21]

It is Picard's desire to do 'the right thing' that gives him the strength to withstand the pain inflicted by Madred and which stops him from giving in to the temptation to give Madred the answer he wants. Here, psychological pain and suffering are shown to be of value.

> The 'other' may be just as one-sided in one way as the ego is another. And yet the conflict between them may give rise to truth and meaning – but only if the ego is willing to grant the other its rightful personality.[22]

Of course, it is a matter of conjecture, but I suspect that Picard does not actually develop much as a result of his devastating experience. His own 'shadow' remains fairly well repressed and locked into the depths of this psyche. It will emerge in later episodes with particularly destructive consequences, most notably in *The Best of Both Worlds Parts 1 & 2*, (TNG) where Picard is transformed into Locutus of Borg and forced to cooperate with the Borg in the destruction of 39 starships and their crews. This view of *Star Trek* is at odds with other more frequent and positive interpretations of the psychological state of characters and cultures in the series. For example, Chris Gregory suggests:

> In *Star Trek* the utopian society on Earth is portrayed as an 'ideal culture' in which every individual can become 'self-actualised'. In the new *Trek* series it is emphasised that Starfleet officers are virtual 'Renaissance' men and women, skilled and educated in many disparate areas.[23]

It is true that Starfleet officers are generally well educated. They are knowledgeable about literature, history, social customs, cuisine and so on. But their education seems lacking in one particular regard – psychology, and almost all the characters seem to lack the capacity for any type of real introspection. (Even Dianna Troi, the ship's counsellor on Enterprise-D, often behaves in a most un-counsellor like fashion.) There is little evidence that the characters can learn from their experiences. Further, their sense of self is clearly defined in relation to the quasi-military structure of Starfleet and any move away from the ethos of the organization risks danger and disaster. This points towards a deep ambivalence that is at the very heart of *Star Trek*. Each series is concerned with the individual, yet there remains a distrust of individuals and an awareness of the capacity for evil that is intrinsic to the human condition. Under no circumstances must an individual surrender their own identity, yet (and here is the contradiction) the crew must conform to Starfleet protocols. This point will be returned to later as it suggests something quite fundamental about the psychological composition of *Star Trek*.

The darkness of *Chain of Command Part 2* contrasts with *The Inner Light* (TNG). This is another episode that is concerned with questions of identity, and it is yet another point at which Picard's body is invaded by an alien technology. The plot line is neatly summarized by Picard at the end of the episode where he describes what has happened to him.

> The *Enterprise* encountered a probe from the planet, before it was destroyed. It scanned me and I lost consciousness. And, in the space of 25 minutes, I live a lifetime on that

planet. I had a wife and children, and a grandchild, and it was absolutely real to me.

Picard – *The Inner Light.*

Picard's new character lives on the planet Kataan where he has become Kamin, an ironweaver, although his main pleasure in life comes from playing his Ressikan flute. (In a piece of neat casting Kamin's son Batai is played by Daniel Stewart, the son of Patrick Stewart, the actor who plays Picard.)

In *The Inner Light* the light is both Picard's and that of the probe. The double meaning of the image implies that the inner sanctum of the self, the sanctuary where the inner light burns, is not a private and isolated place. Deep within Picard is not only the inner light of himself but also the inner light of an entire culture, its hopes, dreams, family structure, and religious mores.... *The Inner Light* serves to remind us that each individual is a crucible of culture. The series may do everything it can to preserve the integrity of the individual, but the individual is integral for a surprising reason. No man is an island because each man is a continent.[24]

Picard (Patrick Stewart) plays a Ressikan Flute in *Inner Light*

Curiously, Picard is able to bring back the Ressikan flute with him and it crops up in subsequent episodes (*Lessons, A Fistful of Datas*, both TNG). It seems as though the probe contained not just memories but also housed the one artefact – one that enabled Picard to connect to a situation through music and through his emotions.

> The story of *The Inner Light* has caught the imagination of many people. This is partly because it represents the historic existence of a society not through empirical information but through the lived memories of one individual. The decision of the Kataans to represent their culture in this way is entirely consistent with *Star Trek*'s insistence that individual experience, in this case transmitted through memory, is the essence of human identity.[25]

For the purposes of this chapter it is possible to interpret the story in a slightly different manner. The idea that the individual can be the repository for collective historical experiences finds a resonance in the Jungian observation that the individual psyche is both personal and collective. Located at the very heart of the person Jung postulated the existence of the objective psyche. This was a metaphor that Jung used to explain the recurrent mythological material that he found in his patients and in his own dreams and creative activities. The objective psyche is composed of fundamental patterns which find expression in images; while the patterns are fixed, the images vary according to personal conditions and cultural pressures – their function is to guide each individual in his or her psychological maturation – what Jung called the processes of individuation. In this way Jung is suggesting that the individual embodies collective aspects. This particular element is often misinterpreted by New Age thinkers to mean that there is a mystical substratum which connects all humankind. This is not quite what Jung was getting at. He was not really interested in the ego losing its sense of self-identity rather as the ego grows in strength he suggests it becomes aware of both its unique qualities and its collective ties and associations.

Related to this is the episode *Frame of Mind* (TNG).[26] It takes place on the planet Tilonus IV, which is in a state of rebellion. Riker attempts to rescue a Federation research team but in doing so he is captured and subjected to mind-manipulation in an attempt to gain tactical information from him. Riker believes that his psychiatrist, Dr Sirus (David Selberg), is a physician who works at the Tilonus Institute for Mental Disorders. However, it transpires that Dr Sirus is a fantasy implanted in Riker's mind by the political interrogation officers on Tilonus IV. The mind manipulation takes on an interesting form and it results in a complex narrative structure which is based around a series of fantasies and illusions, each of which is dissolved only to reveal another fantasy.

As the narrative unfolds it slowly becomes clear that prior to the start of *Frame of Mind*, Riker had been rehearsing a play in which his character was a mental patient with Data as his psychiatrist (it is up to the reader to make up their own mind about whether some comment on psychiatrists is intended). This forms the basis for the fantasy world, which his interrogators create. Riker is encouraged to believe that he is being treated for a mental disorder in which he believes that he is rehearsing a play and that he is an officer

Riker (Jonathan Frakes) Undergoes Reflection Therapy in *Frame of Mind*

on board a Federation Starship. In his fantasy, part of his treatment is something called Reflection Therapy which the *Star Trek Encyclopedia* describes as follows:

> ...[a process] in which the patient's brain is scanned and images from the brain areas that control emotions and memory are projected holographically. The patient then interacts with holographic images, which represent various facets of his personality.[27]

In other words, it is a type of active imagination in which various aspects (archetypes) latent in Riker take on human form. Importantly all this happens as part of the induced fantasy the purpose of which is extract tactical information from Riker. The episode illustrates what can happen if the unconscious takes over. Riker initially believes his fantasies are real, and he is unable to make the distinction between unconscious fantasies and the real situation. It is sometimes mistakenly thought that Jungian psychology advocates exactly this approach, although, in fact, the opposite is true. This confusion partly comes about from one of the precepts of Jungian analysis which is that the situation in the unconscious must be accepted by the analyst as this provides the starting point for the subsequent analysis. If another course of action is followed, the danger is that symptoms, rather than the underlying causes, are treated.

But what people thought they could nonchalantly write off as 'imaginary' is only one manifestation of a morbid state that is positively protean in its symptomatology. No sooner is one symptom suppressed than another is there. The core of the disturbance had not been reached.[28]

However, Jung is not suggesting that we should stay immersed in the mythological world of fantasy that characterizes archetypal expression, as this would place an individual at the beck and call of unconscious archetypal forces. This is certainly not the goal of individuation. In noting the tension the archetypal core of the psyche sets up with consciousness cannot be resolved, Jung suggests something more challenging. At best this tension can be transcended. Through becoming more aware of what lies within the psyche and not attributing it solely to external causes, it is possible to hold together the tensions, they are not resolved.

Again, the view that good and evil are spiritual forces outside us, and that man is caught in the conflict between them, is more bearable by far than the insight that the opposites are the in eradicable and indispensable preconditions of all psychic life, so much so that life itself is guilt.[29]

Riker's imaginary psychiatrist pushes him in this direction and warns him that in Reflection Therapy, 'You'll be interacting with aspects of your psyche you've never dealt with before and you may be disturbed by what they have to say.' Again in the fantasy Troi notes, 'Sometimes it's healthy to explore the darker side of the psyche. Jung called it owning your own shadow...Don't be afraid of your darker side – have fun with it.' But, of course, all these characters are trying to deceive Riker – far from helping him they are the agents of Riker's interrogators. And, thus, Data's observation that 'Most humans have the potential to be irrational. Perhaps you should attempt to access that part of your psyche' seems, as you reflect on the episode, like a trap. What is to be made of this?

Star Trek has a curiously ambivalent attitude to the world of images, storytelling, myth and the unconscious in general. One message that it is possible to take from the episode is that therapy, which encourages a direct confrontation with the unconscious, is a tool that is put to use only by enemies of the Federation in conflict situations – it is by definition, therefore, bad. Another reading sees that the episode actually highlights the importance of fantasy, and images in coming to a realistic appreciation of a situation. It is important to remember that the episode is actually based around a theatrical performance on the Enterprise – it finishes with Riker striking the set, and acknowledgement that its work had been done.The episode's neat title suggests the psyche may be framed in a variety of ways: in 'reflection therapy'; by mind altering drugs; in the fantasy of the theatre; and, by extension, by the television set on which *Star Trek* is watched. What is important is not so much the fantasy as the intention that lies behind it. Fantasy can be good when it understood as a means by which to more fully understand ourselves and engage with reality. This happens in episodes like *Birthright* (TNG) where Worf tells a group of Klingon children, 'These are our stories. They tell us who we are.' Fantasy is bad, when it takes us away from the reality of the world we live in and encourages us to stay in the unconscious as in this particular episode of *Star Trek*.

Conclusion

Thomas Richards has suggested that 'In many ways *Star Trek* is "a space *Illiad*," not "a space *Odyssey*"'.[30] The Odyssey is the story of one man's (Odysseus) attempt to return home after the Trojan War. By contrast, the *Illiad* concerns itself with the differences between the Greeks and the Trojans. But instead of a Mediterranean setting for political intrigue, *Star Trek* has created an ever-expanding universe of planets and races. Richard's concise summary points us toward the central contradiction and tension that lies at the heart of *Star Trek*. On the one hand there is what amounts to Gene Roddenberry's personal Odyssey. His search to find something in himself and in humanity, which is noble, respectable and honourable. Yet, as has been demonstrated, running throughout *Star Trek* there is a deep ambivalence about the value of humanity and this was also reflected in Rodenbury's personal life. In an interview Roddenberry's biographer comments to him, 'You are *Star Trek*. And the TV show is a manifestation of *Star Trek*. A manifestation, in fact, of you?' To which he replies, 'Yes...I really am *Star Trek*.'[31] But he also commented:

> I have a theory about that [the difference between people and humanity]. I call it a socio-organism...When life originated on this planet, it was a single-cell organism. And perhaps by accident, or a need for survival, or some primal urge, these individual cells began to group together to form collectives, then units, then a corporate body. And that's what happens on a larger scale with humans...But if you follow the thought logically, you can project a more complex interaction – perhaps a thinking body in which the individual units no longer function in any capacity as individuals...I think we may be headed that way. It seems to me a natural consequence of evolution.[32]

At the heart of this rests an anxiety about what happens when we loose control and this is a theme that is taken up in numerous episodes of *Star Trek*. Roddenberry tries to make sense of this tension between control and authority, between the individual and collective in mythological terms by quite literally creating his own myth. It turned out to be one that resonated with other people.

> ...Gene fluctuated between the fascination of collective consciousness and a fierce, fatherly protectionism for the independent individual of the human species...he come down rather heavily in public in favour of individualism, hence the sinister threat of the Borg race. Privately, he didn't think it mattered all that much...if there were some cosmic insistence on unification, he believed it would take place as naturally and painlessly slowly as previous evolution.[33]

The standard view of the world of *Star Trek* is of one which offers a utopian future where people coexist in peace, and the higher and better nature of humankind rises to the surface. In fact, Roddenberry's comments confirm the earlier suggestion that there is deep ambivalence at the centre of *Star Trek*, a profound black hole from which no light may escape. This ambivalence about human nature views it as both a force for good and evil and requires both individual and collective elements. Perhaps the need to hold in tension the constant shifts in the psyche between the unconscious and consciousness, between the collective and the individual, is actually the reason why *Star Trek* is so successful. While apparently offering a utopian myth it actually encapsulates the fallen and dark side of the human psyche. To this extent, *Star Trek* is a complex reworking of the creation of myth of Eden. The mythology of the 'fall' forms part of the central quest of humanity to better understand our relation to the word. This reveals its fundamentally dark nature and lost sense of innocence where, despite the sacrifice of individuals to improve the situation for the greater good, the result is failure.

The extent to which Roddenberry was aware of such ideas, and their Jungian resonances is difficult to know. Perhaps as a creative individual he was drawn to some of the same conclusions as Jung but via a rather different route. It certainly seems so when he comments,

> I like the image of impregnation and birth. We men often have difficulty applying those terms to ourselves. But we are all male and female inside. Some people recognise that – especially writers...[34]

Analytical psychology might use slightly different terms, but it shares the same general trajectory in wanting to see sexuality as in terms of similarity and inclusivity rather than difference and separation.

Perhaps the key to understanding the ambivalence that rests at the heart of the *Star Trek* universe, and within Roddenberry himself, lies in two simple questions asked to him by Yvonne Fern; apparently he found difficult to answer. The first was, 'What do you most fear?'. To which Roddenberry eventually answered some hours later, 'Humanity'. Later she asked him, 'What moves you?'. To which Roddenberry more readily replied, 'I would say, it has to be the same answer: humanity'.[35]

Notes

1. Wess, R., and Ross, B. *Make it so: Leadership Lessons from Star Trek: The Next Generation*. (Pocket Books: New York, 1996).
2. Hastie, A. 'Fabricated Space: Assimilating the Individual on *Star Trek: The Next Generation*', in *Enterprise Zones: Critical Positions on Star Trek*. Eds Harrison *et al.* (Westview Press: Boulder, 1996), p. 120.
3. *Ibid.*, p. 122.
4. Jung, C. G. (1963/70) *Collected Works*, vol. 14. (London: Routledge and Kegan Paul), para. 258.
5. Jung, C. G. (1960/69) *Collected Works*, vol. 8. (London: Routledge and Kegan Paul), para. 143.
6. Barrett, M., and Barrett, D. *Star Trek: The Human Frontier*. (Polity: Cambridge, 2001), p. 121.
7. Cf. Hanley, R. *The Metaphysics of Star Trek*. (Basic Books: New York, 1977). Krauss, L. *The Physics of Star Trek*. (Harper Collins: London, 1995). Andreadis, A. *To Seek Out New Life: The Biology of Star Trek*. (Crown Publishers: New York, 1998).
8. Jung, C. G. (1964/71) *Collected Works*, vol. 6. (London: Routledge and Kegan Paul), para. 718.

9. Jung, C. G. (1960/69) *Collected Works*, vol. 8. (London: Routledge and Kegan Paul), para. 618.
10. Jung, C. G. (1964/71) *Collected Works*, vol. 6. (London: Routledge and Kegan Paul), para. 78. Emphasis as original.
11. Jung, C. G. (1958/69) *Collected Works*, vol. 11. (London: Routledge and Kegan Paul), para. 132.
12. Hanna, B. *Encounters with the Soul: Active Imagination as Developed by C. G. Jung.* (Cambridge: Sigo Press, 1981), p. 5.
13. Casement, A. *Jung.* (Sage: London, 2001), p. 95.
14. Admittedly this is a concept which seems somewhat out of vogue currently but which, nonetheless, has some utility here.
15. Jung, C. G. (1953/66) *Collected Works*, vol. 7. (London: Routledge and Kegan Paul), para. 297.
16. Projansky, S. 'When the Body Speaks', in *Enterprise Zones: Critical Positions on Star Trek*. Eds Harrison *et al.* (Westview Press: Boulder, 1996), p. 45.
17. Richards, T. *The Meaning of Star Trek*. (Doubleday: New York, 1997), p. 95.
18. Jung, C. G. (1953/66) *Collected Works*, vol. 7. (London: Routledge and Kegan Paul), para. 267.
19. Jung, C. G. (1964/71) *Collected Works*, vol. 6. (London: Routledge and Kegan Paul), para. 230.
20. Jung, C. G. (1954) *Collected Works*, vol. 17. (London: Routledge and Kegan Paul), para. 319.
21. Jung, C. G. (1953/68) *Collected Works*, vol. 12. (London: Routledge and Kegan Paul), para. 37. Emphasis as original.
22. Jung, C. G. (1959/68) *Collected Works*, vol. 9i. (London: Routledge and Kegan Paul), para. 237.
23. Gregory, C. *Star Trek Parallel Narratives*. (Macmillan: London, 2000), p. 146.
24. Richards, T. *The Meaning of Star Trek*. (Doubleday: New York, 1997), p. 90.
25. Barrett, M., and Barrett, D. *Star Trek: The Human Frontier*. (Polity: Cambridge, 2001), p. 126.
26. Any relationship to the title of this book is, of course, coincidental.
27. Okuda, M. and Okuda, D. with Mirek, D. *The Star Trek Encyclopedia: A Reference Guide to the Future*. (Pocket Books: New York, 1999), p. 403.
28. Jung, C. G. (1964.66) *Collected Works*, vol. 16. (London: Routledge and Kegan Paul), para. 32.
29. Jung, C. G. (1963/70) *Collected Works*, vol. 14. (London: Routledge and Kegan Paul), para. 206.
30. Richards, T. *The Meaning of Star Trek*. (Doubleday: New York, 1997), p. 11.
31. Fern, Y. *Inside the Mind of Gene Roddenberry The Creator of Star Trek*. (HaperCollins: London, 1995), p. 80.
32. *Ibid.*, p. 16.
33. *Ibid.*, p. 22.
34. Fern, Y. *Inside the Mind of Gene Roddenberry The Creator of Star Trek*. (HaperCollins: London, 1995), p. 75.
35. Fern, Y. *Inside the Mind of Gene Roddenberry The Creator of Star Trek*. (HaperCollins: London, 1995), pp. 23–24, pp. 28–29.

7

TECHNOLOGY AS
MODERN MYTH AND MAGIC

This chapter explores Jung's views on the psychological state of western society. It does so as the starting point for a discussion about the role of contemporary communication technologies. Of particular interest are screen-based media such as television, and it will explore the extent to which they repudiate or support Jung's view that life in the contemporary western world is increasingly devoid of psychologically meaningful symbols and activities.

Jung had a particular view about what might be thought of as the 'myth of progress'. This myth is composed of at least two interwoven strands: the first of these concerns the development of society and culture, which by extension includes communications technology; the second consists of consciousness and the awareness of the psyche as it gradually comes to recognize the existence of the unconscious and its effects. Inevitably the two strands cannot easily be disentangled. Indeed at this point it might be wiser to leave the complex interplay of unconscious contents, external social, political and cultural forces and the shifting nature of the ego as it attempts to construct its sense of self. Instead of an unravelling, what is needed is to hold the tension of these differing energies as they are wrapped up in themselves. This does not mean that they are being ignored. Instead, their existence is noted and will be returned to periodically as part of the process of reflecting on how this force field of competing energies comes to influence the psychological and cultural roles of technology.

Jung held to the view that contemporary western society had somehow become divorced from its mythological, some might say spiritual, roots. Jung suggested a number of possible reasons as to why this particular development had come about. Included in these was the failure of mainstream religions to hold on to meaningful symbols. He felt their currency had been debased and replaced with the poverty of symbolic expression deployed by political movements and ideologies. He was also critical of the dominance of the intellectual in the western societies as the dominant mode of enquiry. These concerns surface at regular intervals in Jung's writing and form what might reasonably be regarded as a fairly consistent set of themes throughout his work. This said, in his earlier work such concerns tend to be particularly implicit, which is certainly not the case in his later writing. For example, take this extract from his 1957 commentary on *The Secret of the Golden Flower* (a Chinese alchemical text) – Jung's comments were published just four years before his death.

> Only in the course of the nineteenth century, when spirit began to degenerate into intellect, did a reaction set in against the unbearable dominance of intellectualism, and this led to the unpardonable mistake of confusing intellect with spirit and blaming the latter for the misdeeds of the former. The intellect does indeed do harm to the soul when it dares to possess itself of the heritage of the spirit. It is in no way fitted to do this, for spirit is something higher than intellect since it embraces the latter and includes the feelings as well.[1]

This is one of those slightly confusing pieces of writing which, it has to be said, are not that uncommon from Jung. One reading of the extract might suggest that Jung is downplaying the role of the intellect in favour of a seemingly more mystical sense of 'spirit'. However, a better interpretation of this passage would be to understand that 'spirit' acts as a synonym for psyche. Even though this is clearly not a direct translation, more a transliteration, it is a reasonable assumption to make, as while Jung did not exactly use the terms interchangeably they are nonetheless closely related. This points towards one of the founding principles of the Jungian viewpoint, namely that in and of itself the intellect itself is not enough. There is more to humanity than the intellect, important and indispensable though it is. Jung maintains that rationality and intellectualization are crucial processes in coming to a proper and full understanding of ourselves and our relation to the world. However, he is no less insistent in his assertion that there is a poverty to the intellectual project and that this in turn extends to products of the intellect. The suggestion is that the rise of industrialization in the nineteenth century should be seen as the direct consequence of the development of scientific materialist modes of enquiry. This caused a cultural *volte face* in the historical orientation of western culture. The biblical creation myths were clearly no longer sustainable in the face of Darwin's theory of evolution and other scientific developments, particularly in geology. For the first time new scientific insights revealed clearly that the world had not come into being in the space of a single week. Nor had the human species been made in a single moment and it was, in fact, in a constant state of biological adaptation and development. Therefore, the cultural focus changed from one which looked backwards to a lost state of innocence in the Garden of Eden (a pre-fallen society) to one which looked forward towards the ever improving state of human life, both here on earth and eventually in heaven. The old creation myths had been swept aside and in their place the myth of technological progress was instated, with all the redemptive qualities and salvation this implies. In such concerns, and in his interpretation of the broad sweep of human development, Jung was far from alone. As Peter Homans has pointed out:

> ...it can be observed that the forces of industrialization – particularly urbanization, mass transportation, and mass communications – were extremely threatening to

intellectuals and social critics in the first half of the twentieth century, and Jung clearly thought of himself as a member of this group.[2]

What permeates Jung's writing on this topic is a sense of loss – a sense that the ascendancy of the intellectual has come at a considerable cost. This view is consistent with his general principle that everything psychological is two-faced, which is to say both forward-looking and backward-looking. For Jung, the danger inherent in the intellectual project is that it forgets to look back, and instead tries to live solely in the new myth of progress. Its orientation is towards the future as it conceives of the culture as progressing towards an ever better and more fulfilling state.

> Since the differentiated consciousness of civilised man has been granted an effective instrument for the practical realisation of its contents through the dynamics of his will, there is all the more danger, the more he trains his will, of his getting lost in one-sidedness and deviating further and further from the laws and roots of his being. This means, on the one hand, the possibility of human freedom, but on the other it is a source of endless transgressions against one's instincts...But our progressiveness, though it may result in a great many delightful wish-fulfilments, piles up an equally gigantic Promethean debt which has to paid off from time to time in the form of hideous catastrophes. For ages man has dreamed of flying, and all we got for it is saturation bombing![3]

Jung's exasperation over the lack of understanding of what he conceives as basic psychological principles is clear. For him it is self-evident that the psyche is not composed in an either/or manner. It is not adequate to reduce the complexity of human psychology to simple polar opposites such as good or bad, rational or irrational, neither thinking nor feeling. Instead the psyche is all of these things, and all at once. Yet there still remains a sense in which it is all too easy to pigeonhole Jung as a romantic, as someone who harks back to an age where it was possible to live in harmony with nature and as someone who mourns the passing of a golden naïve age of relatedness to the world. Far from looking to the future for our psychological development it might appear that Jung is advocating a return to a utopian innocence. It is, indeed, quite possible to find echoes of this type of thought in passages of his writing, of which the following is a typical example:

> Modern man has lost all the metaphysical certainties of his medieval brother, and set up in their place the ideals of material security, general welfare and humanitarianism. But anyone who has still managed to preserve these ideals unshaken must have been injected with a more than an ordinary dose of optimism. Even security has gone by the board, for modern man has begun to see that every step forward in material 'progress' steadily increases the threat of a still more stupendous catastrophe. The imagination shrinks in terror from such a picture.[4]

However, as suggested above, to limit Jung's world-view to that of the romantic would be an error as Jung also maintained that it is no bad thing that modern man has lost his medieval metaphysical certainties. Indeed, his view was that it was inevitable. What

Jung was trying to do was to reveal what had been lost. He does so not with the intention of advocating a return to such values, partly because it would be impossible, but also because it is for each age and culture to find for itself the best way it can of making sense of the world. For Jung, history becomes a metaphor through which to better understand our psychological relationship to the world. Analytical psychology therefore is, at its heart, a way of engaging with the world. It seeks not to withdraw from it, or retreat into its past, but to encounter it and transform it. Individuation is not about shutting out the world. Its intention is quite the opposite, for individuation is about the acceptance of our collective responsibilities and ties. It involves accepting our past, while not necessarily retreating into it.

Jung clearly thought that individuals, through their own psychological development, also help the wider culture at large to develop and change. Perhaps this is one of the marked differences between analytical psychology and its counterpart, psychoanalysis.

> Jung sought to revitalize contemporary culture, which – he believed – had lost its anchorage in the past, by relinking that culture to its past (especially the mythic past) with the assistance of depth psychology, and he worked within the assumptive world of Christian humanism. In contrast, Freud wanted to break decisively with the past, by unmasking it with depth psychology (what I called culture-analyzing), in the interest of a new beginning in Western culture, and he worked within the assumptive world of modern science.[5]

For Jung, analytical psychology became his contribution to broader psychological debates. Perhaps more importantly for him it was also his way of facing up to the personal challenge of finding something that could redress the imbalance inherent in the dominance of the intellectual and rational world. In doing so Jung often described his own work as 'scientific' or 'empirical' and insisted that he only believed what he 'knew', yet analytical psychology goes in quite a different direction to that suggested by those terms. In reality his aim was to provide a new way to articulate and experience the act of 'being'. For Jung, analytical psychology was a response to the growing dominance of an increasingly industrialized and technological world. It provided an integrative method through which it was possible to reconnect the psyche to the lost parts of itself.

> It remained for modern science to despiritualise nature through its so-called objective knowledge of matter. All anthropomorphic projections were withdrawn from the object one after another, with a twofold result: firstly man's mystical [unconscious] identity with nature was curtailed as never before, and secondly the projections falling back into the human soul [psyche] caused such a terrific activation of the unconscious that in modern times man was compelled to postulate the existence of an unconscious psyche. The first beginnings of this can be seen in Leibniz and Kant, and then, with mounting intensity, in Schelling, Carus, and von Hartmann, until finally modern psychology discarded the last metaphysical claims of the philosopher-psychologists and restricted the idea of the psyche's existence to the psychological statement, in other words, to phenomenology.[6]

Jung could at times also put the situation even more prosaically. Even if the tone in the following quote is rather different the point remains the same; that there is a sense in which psychology takes up the mantle of religion. (It should not be forgotten that psychotherapy means, care of the soul.)This is not to say that Jungian psychology is substitute religion, although there are those who have levelled this charge at Jung.[7] Rather, Jung offers up a new vocabulary with a fresh psychological system, which has the capacity to offer a greater degree of consciousness than before.

> All ages before us have believed in gods in some form or other. Only an unparalleled impoverishment of symbolism could enable us to rediscover the gods as psychic factors, that is, as archetypes of the unconscious. No doubt this discovery is hardly credible at present. To be convinced, we need to have the experience pictured in the dream of the theologian, for only then do we experience the self-activity of the spirit moving over the waters. Since the stars have fallen from heaven and our highest symbols have paled, a secret life holds sway in the unconscious. That is why we have a psychology today, and why we speak of the unconscious. All this would be quite superfluous in an age or culture that possess symbols.[8]

Typically of Jung, he tries to hold together a series of tensions within the psyche as a way of containing their opposing convictions. (Alternatively, it is possible to say that he attempts to transcend such tension.) For him, the psyche is introverted and extraverted, rational and non-rational and it also looks both forward and backwards. Put another way, the psyche is teleological but this is no mere straightforward linear trajectory. The goal is the development of the Self, the fuller understanding of us as individuals and discovering (in a psycho-historical and familial sense) where we have come from. It is this process which Jung terms individuation. In this regard, Jung does not have in mind an understanding of just our personal life experience and family upbringing, important though these are. Instead he envisages a psyche which, as part of its unique and personal formation, understands its cultural and psychological heritages as well. In so doing, Jung is claiming that ultimately everything has a psychological heritage. Peter Homans puts it as follows:

> He [Jung] did indeed counsel a return to the past, yet only so that the past might be surpassed. The modern ego must, as it were, travel through the past, on its way to the future. If individuation is allowed to continue uninterrupted, the assimilation of the archetypes of the collective unconscious results in the formation of the self, a core of essential, personal uniqueness that exists beyond institutions and roles – in short, a truly meta-institutional self. As such, the self cannot be defined entirely in terms of conformity either to modernity or to tradition; it constitutes a genuinely new structure, not simply an amalgam of the two. The Jungian self assimilates the past, by means of the archetypes, but it also repudiates it, for it 'sees through' the claims of tradition by penetrating to their archetypal infrastructure.[9]

Having established Jung's views on the development of western industrialized society it is now a good point to shift direction and develop a psychological view of technology. This brings into focus Jung's view that technology is part of the discourse of rationalistic materialism. It also suggests the possibility of relocating technology in a different, and all together more mythological, discourse. The focus in the next part of this chapter will be on communications technology and specifically on the closely related qualities of television and the computer monitor. The suggestion is that when such technology is approached from the perspective of depth psychology, it is evident that the worlds of myth and scientific rationalism are not as separate as they might appear.

From the preceding discussion it might be reasonable to anticipate that Jung would find in technology something beneficial but also something to be concerned about. In fact, he is fairly consistent in his condemnation of technology. He regards it as one of the unpleasant by-products of a rationalist and materialist world-view. As such technology, for Jung, serves to further the process of disconnecting us from ourselves and in so doing sap us of the energy that is needed to deal with the real problems of life.

> In general it can be said that for modern man technology is an imbalance that begets dissatisfaction with work or with life. It estranges man from his natural versatility of action and thus allows many of his instincts to lie fallow. The result is an increased resistance to work in general.[10]

Despite this somewhat negative view of technology Jung did in fact recognize that technology could have an archetypal, or to scale this down a little, a psychological dimension. In his well-known article *Flying Saucers: A Modern Myth of Things Seen in the Skies* Jung examines how the psychological desire for religiosity and salvation is projected upward (the traditional home of the gods, after all); only on this occasion the project assumes the form of a UFO. Like astrology, the myth of the flying saucer suggests that the stars, or something from the stars, at least, can alter life here on earth.

While in the following quote Jung is specifically referring to that context, his comments remain pertinent to our broader discussion:

> It is characteristic of our time that the archetype, in contrast to its previous manifestations, should now take the form of an object, a technological construction, in order to avoid the odiousness of mythological personification. Anything that looks technological goes down without difficulty with modern man.[11]

Again, a couple of points of clarification are in order. When Jung writes of the 'odiousness of mythological personification' he is, of course, referring to western rationalism's perception of mythology and not mythology *per se*. Nor do his comments mitigate against viewing technology as part of mythological system of meaning. Indeed, behind the observation that an object of technological construction, a UFO, for example, is the manifestation of an archetype comes the implicit assumption that the products of technology are indeed part of broader systems of meaning. Put differently, they are part of a contemporary mythology. Robert Romanyshyn in *Technology as Symptom and Dream* develops this point:

In building a technological world we create ourselves, and through the events which comprise this world we enact and live out our experiences of awe and wonder, our fantasies of service and of control, our images of exploration and destruction, our dreams of hope and nightmares of despair.[12]

Thus, the technical world of mass media communications comes to be part of a mythological space, a space which is as likely to be the recipient of unconscious projections as any other person, object, place and so on. Interestingly, and crucially different to the environment of individual clinical analysis is that these fantasies are played out on a global scale as shared anxieties, hopes, frustrations and fears. As the following passage shows, Jung was certainly of the opinion that collective expressions of unconscious material were of importance. He also clearly noted this type of collective psychological material could find its way into literary and other mediated texts, not just as the result of the author or production team but as in someway coming to be embodiment of collective unconscious material. (Here is the context for a quote used earlier in this book.)

I must plead guilty, however, to the charge of one-sidedness, for I have passed over in silence the spirit of the times, about which everyone has so much to say because it is so clearly apparent to us all. It shows itself in the ideal of internationalism and supernationalism, embodied in the League of Nations and the like; we see it also in sport and, significantly, in cinema and jazz. These are characteristic symptoms of our time, which has extended the human ideal even to the body. Sport puts an exceptional valuation on the body, and this tendency is emphasized still further in modern dancing. The cinema, like the detective story, enables us to experience without danger to ourselves all the excitements, passions, and fantasies which have to be repressed in a humanistic age. It is not difficult to see how these symptoms link up with our psychological situation.[13]

Such 'symptoms' are seen every day in the mass media. Previous chapters examined in some detail how advertising and other popular media texts use mythological material, sometimes intentionally and sometimes unknowingly. It does not take a great leap to see how this premise can be extended to other media and forms. The news, for example, is redolent with mythological imagery as suggested by the press's treatment of Lady Diana Spencer as fairy-tale Princess, or the use of green man myths through which to report stories on ecology.[14] However Jung's claims that it is 'not difficult to see how these symptoms link up with our psychological situation' is, certainly for the non-clinician, less self-evident; while such symptoms may indeed reveal something of the psychological state of society, interpreting their significance may not prove to be quite as simple as Jung suggests. Romanyshyn is right to remind us that, 'Whatever else technology does, therefore, it does indicate that events are also images and that images are events in the world'.[15]

At this point it is important to remember that, for Jung, images from the unconscious have two related roles. Firstly they state the psychological situation as it is, secondly they attempt to keep the psyche in a homeostatic state. This is a somewhat different model to that proposed by psychoanalysis, which sees images (primarily dream images) as an expression of unconscious complexes that have to be decoded if their intended meanings are to be revealed. The dream work of condensation, displacement and visualization encrypts the unpalatable psychological truth in culturally acceptable terms. It is the work of analysis to help the patient break the code, remove the repression and in so doing to discover the root problem, however culturally and socially unacceptable it may be.

Jung proposed an alternative psychological mechanism in which the unconscious behaves much like the rest of the human body. He suggests that the psyche has a natural tendency toward both health and growth. As such when 'sick' the psyche attempts to heal itself in a manner which is akin to the body's physiological activities. It does so by releasing images (sometimes as dreams and sometimes in other forms) along with other psychological 'symptoms', that have the capacity to reveal what is happening. In so doing, the psyche attempts to promote healing and growth with imagery that compensates for any psychological imbalance in consciousness.

In summary, images both tell us what is going on in the psyche, both personal and collective, and they also have the potential to offer an insight into cultural and psychological attitudes. This position is not so different to that offered by some sociological approaches, nor indeed from some media theories, where the emphasis tends to be on how otherness is defined in relation to social norms. The American communications theorist John Peters has come at this issue from a different approach that, while its origins are outside depth psychology, is nonetheless sympathetic towards a psychological reading of media communications:

> Questions about the inhuman – nature, machines, animals, extraterrestrials – often serve as allegories of social otherness – women, racial and sexual others, the insane, children, the senile, or one's own dear self. Today communication is the preeminent field for carrying out the command, Know Thyself.[16]

Clearly this perspective has a strong resonance with the psychological point of view. However, in claiming that images in the media of 'otherness' have the capacity to tell us something about ourselves, the psychological attitude goes further down the road of personal discovery of the self than communications theory is normally prepared to. It is important to remember that here it is images that are at work. It has been stressed throughout this book that this approach towards working with images has seen them not in literal concrete terms. Instead, they are regarded as metaphors with sets of negotiated meanings that are brought into existence through the interplay of conscious and unconscious dynamics – an interplay is laden with the energy of affect. While images have an iconic relationship to the world, their hermeneutic value lies in their role as indices of meaning. When an inner image finds itself projected onto the outer world, and going unrecognized as such, the experience of the affect is disproportionately large in relation to the experience. It is not difficult to see how when inner gets confused with outer, and the catalyst of affect comes into play, situations can become inflamed as the rational self momentarily loses control. In part, this is why it is possible to have strong reactions to images that move us at a basic and instinctual level. The meaning is fleeting, cannot be recaptured, but the results of the affect can remain a lot longer. If not recognized, they continue to be experienced leaving individuals once again uncertain about what has happened and why.

On reflection, this is a fairly strange state of affairs as it suggests that something without a physical presence, something that is lacking in an actual form nonetheless has a psychological meaning and value. Peters suggests that far from being unusual this turns out to be intrinsic to the act of communication. It might be argued that he is referring only to technologically mediated communication, but all communication involves a type of technology – the technology of the psyche is not without its art, craft and technique. It is not without structure, dynamic and effect, however metaphorically we might want to regard such qualities.

> Communication suggests touch without contact. To talk on a telephone is to identify an acoustic effigy of the person with an embodied presence. In 'communication' the bodies of the communicants no longer hold the incontrovertible tokens of individuality or personality. Our faces, actions, voices, thoughts, and transactions have all migrated into media that can disseminate the *indicia* of our personhood without our permission. Communication has become disembodied.[17]

This talk, of inner and outer, of bodies and disembodiment seems to suggest a somewhat dualistic approach. As hinted above, in reality these distinctions are not as clear-cut as they might first appear. Image, as the key channel of communication, contains within it both conscious and unconscious elements. The interaction between subject, or in terms of mediated communication between viewer or listener, brings a clear element of subjectivity to the entirety of the process. Meanings are not intentionally inscribed into the image, as might be the case with the psychoanalytic view. They are not manifest content from which the latent content needs to be teased out with a view to exposing the unconscious mechanisms of the psyche. Rather the image as the conveyor of meaning becomes the subject of negotiation and represents the unfolding and encapsulation of meaning at any given moment.

However, certain branches of the philosophical and psychological thought are not convinced by the suggestion that there is value in the idea of an unconscious, nor indeed that terms such as psyche actually have any relevance. Certainly from the perspective of existentialist psychotherapy, with its phenomenological approach to human behaviour, the distinctions between inner and outer and between conscious and unconscious are simply not necessary. All there is, they argue, is 'being in the world'. There is a state of 'being' in which we are aware of some matters and not aware of others and the notion of unconscious agency is for them an encumbrance. They argue that it seems a needlessly complicated way of conceiving human behaviour and that it offers little by way of clarification about the nature of the human condition. Indeed, it can be argued, that such psychodynamic language is arcane, obfuscatory and serves to perpetuate a psychotherapeutic elitist terminology which is outside the reach and criticism of the client. One of the functions of the specialist terminology is to ensure that power and authority rests clearly with the analyst. Along with maintaining the strictures of the therapeutic frame (time, setting, payment, frequency of sessions and the like) the analyst maintains control over the language which the client uses to describe their life experiences. This, it is argued, maintains power, clearly in the hands of the analyst and any attempt by client to seize it for themselves is seen as hostile, aggressive, defensive and generally an attempt by the client to attack the analyst. As such, it is all grist to the analytic mill.

There is some validity to this argument. This is particularly the case in the attention it draws to the power relationships that exist in therapy and the value that is attributed to them. Even so, it remains important not to lose sight of the complexity of the psyche and to remember that meanings should be negotiated not imposed. Any interpretation be it of a film, television programme or encounter between therapist and client, is the result of interaction whose intention is to make meaning. However legitimate the concerns of phenomenology might be, to speak just of 'being in the world' emphasizes notions of individual freedom, of individual concerns and anxieties. The issue is that in doing so it does not take sufficient account of the more intricate interactions that take place between biology, culture, environment, setting, family and so forth. Focusing on the individual means that the no less important roles played by social environment and cultural context are not sufficiently addressed. It is an interesting paradox that a psychological system which sets out to explore 'being' finds utility in philosophical modes of enquiry. For whatever the value of the approach there can be little question that, certainly in terms of justification and the rational, it places a greater stress on intellect than other forms of psychotherapy. As such, it seems overly thinking-focused, which is clearly odd in a mode of engagement which aims to overcome the problematic of dualism. This said, some phenomenological writing attempts to form something of a half-way house and tries to find ways of preserving Jung's ideas of individuation, imperfection and wholeness.

> Jung's vision, while focusing on 'wholeness,' still emanated from the ground of modernism, leaving the world as 'outer' and inanimate. In so far as he emphasised a concealed interior personality as the dwelling place for symbolic life, he maintained the subjectivist split between inner and outer. This mode of thinking, founded on a dualism that interiorises inherent life or 'soul' and externalises the world as culture, technology and nature, is actually an adaptation to a fractured collective consciousness. Culture is seen as 'impacting' analysis which, in turn, is considered as the true agent of change. Cultural factors are imagined as influences on the 'psychological development,' 'dynamics,' and 'identity' of the individual as interior being. Psychological life is 'within' the individual, with the forces of a dead, material world impinging from 'without.' Culture and psyche are opposed, and 'care of the soul,' or psychotherapy, is an 'inner' work which affects the 'outer' world.[18]

But some post-Jungians have also drawn attention to how the outer-world can help shape, influence and interpret the outer world. Most notably Andrew Samuels in *The Political Psyche* explores how analytical psychology can help to understand and contribute to the process of political change but also how the language and imagery (we might say 'mythology', although Samuels does not) of politics is of relevance in the analytic setting. Once again, it is not a question of either/or, but of both – of holding together in a creative tension different perspectives and processes to gain a better understanding and insight.

> The ideas that psyche does not recognise the distinction of 'within' and 'without' and that the world is alive, follow in the tradition of *anima mundi* held by native cultures, ancient Greeks, the alchemists of the Middle Ages, and the Neo-Platonists of the Renaissance. *Anima mundi* or the soul of the world is that life which emanates through all perceptible forms. The natural world and the world of technology, as well as the world of dreams and fantasises, have a life of their own. Things of the world show forth their face in their appearance, and in doing so, reveal their depth. Divinity is at work in the machine as well as in the dream.[19]

So, is there a 'divinity' at work in the television or computer monitor? Surely, this is a ridiculous notion but, allowing for the fact that flies in the face of common sense, some commentators have suggested something along these lines. Goethals' 1981 book, *The TV Ritual: Worship at the Video Altar*, explored how television in the USA partly replaces the roles of more traditional institutions in providing meaningful, if sometimes seemingly trivial, symbols. In part, Goethals is drawn to the expressive quality of television while at the same time he remains wary of the ability of soap operas and sport in particular to anæsthetize the human spirit. Instead of concerning ourselves with specific content, perhaps there is something about the nature of the technology itself which can point us towards the mythology of television.

Television needs electricity to work, to bring it to life if you will, and this simple observation sets us on a road that is both technological and mythological. This simple observation finds a mythological analogue in the idea electricity can re-animate and this is a fantasy that has a long heritage in myth, literature and films. There is something numinous about electricity and the reason for this can be found in classical myth and legend.

For example, Zeus (son of Cronus and Rhea, king of the gods and goddesses) was a weather god and he could create thunderstorms complete with lightning and rain. Theocritus wrote *circa* 265 BCE: 'sometimes Zeus is clear, sometimes he rains'. In Homer's epic poem, *The Iliad*, he used thunderstorms as a weapon against his enemies. The name Zeus is related to the Greek word *dios*, meaning 'bright' as in the brightness of flashes of lightening. His other attributes included the sceptre, the eagle and his *aegis* (the goat skin of Amaltheia which when shaken produced storms and tempests). His lightening bolts are not derived from natural sources, rather they were forged by the Cyclopes for Zeus as a gift after he freed them from the bonds to which they had been fettered by Cronus.

In *Frankenstein*, Shelley used both the new sciences of chemistry and electricity and the older Renaissance tradition of the alchemists' search for the elixir of life to conjure up the Promethean possibility of reanimating the bodies of the dead. Of course, it is electricity that creates the spark of life in Mary Shelley's *Frankenstein*. There remains something magical about magnetism and the invisible lines of force which run from pole to pole. That breaking a magnet in two creates two whole new magnets each with the polar opposites is remarkable. It is no surprise that numerous films have explored the imaginative possibility that television sets or radio signals might be channels through which it is possible to connect to other dimensions and to alien planets (*TerrorVision*, 1986 and the *Dr Who* episode *The Idiot's Lantern* in which Maureen Lipman's plays The Wire – an alien who communicates through television sets) or through which to contact the dead (*White Noise*, 2005 and *Poltergeist*, 1982). Schenk puts it as follows:

> To help further make the imaginal leap connecting television and spirit, we might look at the history of inter-relationship between spirit and electricity. Electricity has been associated with spirit and divinity from the beginning of recorded time. Zeus was thought to cast his thunderbolts as a form of divine judgement.[20]

It is the contention of Robert Romanyshyn that some of this supernatural quality extends to our everyday experience of watching television. If this seems to come out of the blue, then it is worth remembering that cinema as an entertainment partly finds its roots in the dioramas of the mid-nineteenth century. Invented by Daguerre (who would later be the co-inventor of the daguerreotype – a precursor of modern chemical photography), the dioramas were housed in specially built theatres with an audience capacity in the region of 350 people. During the show sophisticated lighting effects gradually changed a landscape painting making it appear that viewers were looking at a natural scene. A still earlier optical entertainment was the phantasmagoria which originated in France in the late eighteenth century. During this 'supernatural' experience ghosts, demons skeletons and the like were projected via a moving magic lantern on to walls and rear projection screens.

> Those images of light which dance on the screen before me always seem miraculous, however much I may understand the explanations for how television works. They are, if truth be told, more like ghosts come to visit and perhaps, depending on one's turn of mind, to haunt us in our isolation. Our explanations in fact can desensitise us to the magic of technology. They can fill us with a false sense of understanding which robs us of the *awe-ful* experience which technology provides, for in fact the experience of living in a technological world fills us with awe in spite of our explanations.[21]

Without doubt there are excesses in Jungian thinking that can have the result of pushing matters just that little bit too far. Giving free range to the processes of amplification means that it is all too easy to enter into that liminal territory where the unconscious laps upon the shores of consciousness. Yet even here, while the rational part of the psyche may resort to ridicule and the defences of intellectual rigour there remains something curiously appealing about the mythological speculations of Schenk. No matter how seemingly at odds with our rational reality the unconscious is, there remains a tenuous connection, a hook if it is preferred, with which the unconscious attempts to pull consciousness back to the mythological underbelly of its existence. The following quote is offered by way of speculation in playful, and trickster-like, manner.

The light of television is not the clear, bright, sunlight of Apollo, however. It takes on more of the quality of the glow for his equally far-shooting sister, the moon goddess, Artemis. We might say that the soft light of television is a form of 'moonshine,' with television-watching taking on the aspect of moon-gazing, peering into a mist, or being drawn toward the feminine mysteries.[22]

This chapter has attempted to present a new way in which to reflect on the role that technology plays. Normally technology is seen as part of a dualist discourse in which technology and the sciences are positioned on one side and magic, superstition and myth on the other. The perspective of depth psychology, and specifically analytical psychology, see the relationship in a more uroboric manner. The uroboros is the image of an animal, often a dragon, eating its own tail. In so doing, it exists in a moment of continuous death and re-creation. Perhaps technology and mythology exist not as separate ends of the body of culture but side-by-side, creating, destroying and re-creating each other in a constant and dynamic process.

Notes

1. Jung, C. G. (1968) *Collected Works* vol. 13. (London: Routledge and Kegan Paul), para. 7.
2. Homans P. *Jung in Context: Modernity and the Making of a Psychology.* (Chicago: University of Chicago Press, 1979), p. 182.
3. Jung, C. G, (1959/68) *Collected Works* Vol. 9i. (London: Routledge and Kegan Paul) .para. 276.
4. Jung, C. G, (1964/70) *Collected Works* Vol. 10. London: (Routledge and Kegan Paul). para. 163.
5. Homans P. *Jung Context: Modernity and the Making of a Psychology.* (Chicago: University of Chicago Press, 1979), p. xliii.
6. Jung, C. G. (1958/69) *Collected Works* vol. 11. (London: Routledge and Kegan Paul), para. 375.
7. The best known of such accusers is Richard Noll who sets out his case in *The Aryan Christ: The Secret Life of Carl Gustav Jung.* (London: Macmillan, 1997) and *The Jung Cult: Origins of a Charismatic Movement.* (Princeton: Princeton University Press, 1994). For a robust rebuttal cf. Sonu Shamdasani's *Cult Fictions: C.G. Jung and the Founding of Analytical Psychology.* (London: Routledge, 1998).
8. Jung, C. G. (1959/68) *Collected Works* vol. 9i. (London: Routledge and Kegan Paul), para. 50.
9. Homans P. *Jung Context: Modernity and the Making of a Psychology.* (Chicago: University of Chicago Press, 1979), p. 204.
10. Jung, C. G. (1976) *Collected Works* vol.18. (London: Routledge and Kegan Paul), para. 1405.
11. Jung, C. G. (1964/70) *Collected Works* vol. 10. (London: Routledge and Kegan Paul), para. 624.
12. Romanyshyn, R. *Technology as Symptom and Dream.* (London: Routledge, 1989), p. 10.
13. Jung, C. G. (1964/70) *Collected Works* vol. 10. (London: Routledge and Kegan Paul), para. 195.

14. Cf. Haynes, J., and Shearer, A. (eds) *When a Princes Dies: Reflections from Jungian Analysts*. (London: Harvest, 1998). I am indebted to James Anslow for the observation about the green man myth.
15. Romanyshyn, R. *Technology as Symptom and Dream*. (London: Routledge, 1989), p. 6.
16. Peters, J, D. *Speaking into the Air: A History of the Idea of Communication*. (Chicago: University of Chicago Press, 1999), p. 229.
17. *Ibid.*, p. 228.
18. Schenk, R. *Spirit in the Tube: The Life of Television* in *Pathways into the Jungian World: Phenomenology and Analytical Psychology* ed. Brooke, R. (London: Routledge, 2000), pp. 85–6.
19. *Ibid.*, p. 86.
20. Schenk, R. *Spirit in the Tube: The Life of Television* in *Pathways into the Jungian World: Phenomenology and Analytical Psychology* ed. Brooke, R. (London: Routledge, 2000), p. 98.
21. Romanyshyn, R. *Technology as Symptom and Dream*, (London: Routledge, 1989), p. 1.
22. Schenk, R. *Spirit in the Tube: The Life of Television* in *Pathways into the Jungian World: Phenomenology and Analytical Psychology* ed. Brooke, R. (London: Routledge, 2000), pp. 96–7.

8

Identity and the Internet

The previous chapter suggested that technology and mythology were not, as is often thought, separate entities. It suggested that there is an *enantiodromaic* linkage between the two, where far from being distinct, in fact, they flow into each other. This was characterized as an uroboric movement. Seeing technology from a mythological perspective begins to relocate it as a means through which meaning is made. It shifts it from the semiotic to the hermeneutic. This chapter builds on those previous observations in order to explore something of our cultural relationship to the Internet. In so doing it examines questions of identity, cultural anxiety, creativity and our relationship to a virtual world.

Clearly the World Wide Web is an important technological event. Arguably its impact in terms of economic patterns of distribution, access to information, ownership, participation and the changes it is making to societal structures is greater than any previous medium. But instead of engaging in a cultural/economic analysis what happens if the Web is viewed from a psychological perspective? On one hand the Web provides new sources of information and unparalleled opportunities for communication yet, at the same time, some are afraid of its dark corners and of its power to corrupt through the easy access it provides to pornography, for example. Others find not corruption but liberation in this aspect of the Web. Our cultural attitude to the Web is also a psychological one. We are both drawn to it and afraid of it. As such it mirrors our relationship to the unconscious aspects of the psyche.

As explored in detail in earlier chapters of this book, one of the principles of Jungian psychology is that images, cultural and personal, reveal something about the psychological state of the person or society that has produced them. So too with the World Wide Web cultures converge, myths and images melt into one another and new ways of explaining, understanding, subverting and polarizing interests emerge. In effect the Web provides a new image of society and as such represents something other than just its surface content – it is more than just denotative. Indeed, in Chapters Two and Three of this book it was argued that the denotative value of an image is relatively unimportant. What matters is the negotiation that takes place between the screen and the viewer; it is in that imaginal and liminal space, in the void between viewer and screen, that the new and living image comes into being which holds the meaning and reality of the situation.

In terms of Jungian psychology this process can usefully be thought of as a creative fantasy. For Jung, fantasy is not used to suggest that something is untrue. In traditional psychoanalytic theory, fantasy is a device used by the psyche through which to escape from the impossibility of the current situation and to imagine what it would be like to escape the confines of the superego and act out our impulses. By contrast, Jung thought fantasy played a key role in the psyche. Remember that dreams (an act of fantasy by any standard) lead not to the revealing of impossible desires but instead they state the situation in the unconscious as it is. It therefore follows that fantasy is a meaning-making action of the psyche and as such it is partly collective and partly personal. As Jung comments:

> It is in *creative fantasies* that we find the unifying function we seek. All the functions that are active in the psyche converge in fantasy...Fantasy has its own irreducible value, for it is a psychic function that has its roots in the conscious and the unconscious alike, in the individual as much as in the collective.[1]

For Jung the roots of fantasy are in the unconscious. While fantasies will relate to conscious life and indeed provide a way though which to understand reality, it is important that they are seen as primarily unconscious. Even if the fantasy is populated with figures that resemble people in the world, in the fantasy they stand for inner aspects of ourselves. This is going to prove important in coming to an understanding of the relationship between the online user and the world he or she encounters on their computer screens.

At different points in the collected works, Jung uses the terms individuality and identity in slightly different ways. However, to all intents and purposes the terms are treated by him as synonymous. As might be anticipated in a psychology which is concerned with the containment of opposing aspects of the psyche, individuality turns out to have a strong collective component.

> As I have already pointed out, individuality reveals itself primarily in the particular selection of those elements of the collective psyche which constitute the persona. These components, as we have seen, are not individual but collective. It is only their combination, or the selection of a group already combined in a pattern, that is individual.[2]

The idea that it is through the selection of collective qualities a unique sense of the individual is formed, seems to resonate with how the Internet is used. Some use it to pay bills, book holidays, create family genealogies. Others trace old friends, forge new friendships and even create new personalities and lives in virtual worlds for themselves. While such new identities are formed online they are nonetheless created from within given sets of information. This process of identity formation is one of collage and combination rather than creation from scratch. For example, in *Second Life* (one of the most popular virtual reality worlds on the Internet), users get to choose from sets of pre-existing characters and icons – what they do with these identities, of course, is not so prescribed.

This said, the division between the collective and the individual is not quite as clear-cut as it might at first seem. The reason for this is that the individual is an embodiment of the collective. Jung thought our individual identities were formed in the interplay between the unconscious archetypal patterns that structure the psyche and experience of the outside world. The challenge is to stay close to the unconscious and to be aware of how it influences our life. Yet at the same time it is crucial to have a strong and stable sense of our individual selves for without that we would be submerged in the unconscious. Previous chapters have explored how cinema and television provide opportunities for us to experience something of the collective in our unique interactions with programmes and films that are watched. Perhaps something of this is also true of the way the Internet is used. On the one hand is a collective object that is external to the psyche while on the other hand this virtual world is invested and appropriated in a manner that is highly personal and individual. Jung is adamant that such a separation is an illusion as it is precisely the interaction between the personal and the collective that understanding is made. So too, the Web is both real and virtual. In earlier chapters the activity was referred to as image-making. Jung comments:

> It is quite simply impossible to effect a clear division of the individual from the collective, and even if it were possible it would be quite pointless and valueless for our purpose. It is sufficient to know that the human psyche is both individual and collective, and that its well-being depends on the natural co-operation of these two apparently contradictory sides. Their union is essentially an irrational life process that can, at most, be described in individual cases, but can neither be brought about, nor understood, nor explained rationally.[3]

There are two principle dangers between which the individual needs to negotiate. The first is that it is possible to deny the existence of the collective aspect to the psyche. To do so is dangerous as this is the part of the psyche which regulates and balances the homeostatic system of well-being and self-development. The second danger is to become immersed in the unconscious to such an extent that it is not possible to distinguish illusion from reality. A version of this occurs when viewers and readers become immersed in the world of a film, reading a novel or in surfing the Net and so forth. It would be quite possible to imagine a condition where an online world, for example, is seemingly more real than the actual world. One line of argument would be to say that this is an essentially harmless activity, and providing no one is getting hurt in the process where is the danger? But Jung cautions against this attitude of mind. He suggests that objects (be they person or experience) can have a redemptive quality. When this happens the libidinal energy of the psyche is attached to the 'object' itself. This is an unhelpful state of affairs as the psychological energy is directed away from the self, where it is needed and is instead attached to the object. Put another way, the formation of the image through which meaning is structured and negotiated has become overly identified with the object, and this reduces the meaning-value of the image. In order for meaning to be restored the identification needs to be broken to reinstate the tension between consciousness and the unconsciousness which is characteristic of the psyche.

> An over-accentuated, 'magical' object orients the subject's consciousness in the direction of the object and thwarts any attempt at individual differentiation, which would obviously have to set in with the detachment of the imago from the object....The detachment of the imagos that give the objects their exaggerated significance restores to the subject that split-off energy which he urgently needs for his own development.[4]

This provides another example of how indispensable the notion of opposition is in analytical psychology. Indeed, it could be argued with its interest in the running together of opposites (*enantiodromia*), the combining of opposites (*coniunctio*) and the identity of opposites (*coincidentia oppositorum*), that analytical psychology is in no small part a psychology of opposites. Adding weight to this is Jung's view that the psyche is constantly in a state of regulation and adjustment that is bought about by the compensatory roles that opposites have within the psyche. Clearly this view of opposites is not constructed around notions of exclusion or inclusion. Rather it sees such activity as the inevitable result of the different parts of the psyche as they coexist. As Jung noted towards the end of his life, '...the opposites are the ineradicable and indispensable preconditions for all psychological life...'[5] Such views see the psyche as partly composed of elements that are in tension with each other, and that not only will this state of affairs not ease, it is actually essential. Put simply, the overarching opposition is between what is consciousness (what we know about ourselves) and what is unconscious (what remains unknown about ourselves).

The notion of archetype is a psychosomatic concept, in that it is a way of understanding the connections that exist between the objective psyche (the unconscious) and the realm of ego-consciousness. As such the body itself has a similar hermeneutic to the image. The body becomes the container for the 'image' which is a result of the interaction between the forces of consciousness and the unconscious. After all, such a somatic concept could hardly be expressed in another form. Perhaps the out-of-body-ness of Internet identities provides a clue as to why such an experience might prove attractive, but also why it proves satisfying. In such a world we are not tied to our psychical bodies or pre-judged because of the way they look. Neither are our accents, social class, education and so forth obvious. In losing the body, the embodied experience of our life is also lost, albeit temporarily, as it will be there waiting our return to the corporeal world.

> The collective psyche must be contrasted with...the concept of *individuality*. The individual stands, as it were, between the conscious part of the collective psyche and the unconscious part. He is the reflecting surface in which the world of consciousness can perceive its own unconscious, historical image, even as

Schopenhauer says that the intellect holds up a mirror to the universal Will. Accordingly, the individual would be a point of intersection or a dividing line, neither conscious nor unconscious, but a bit of both.[6]

The proposition is that in interacting with online media the body is temporarily rendered unimportant (other than for the functional acts of typing and using a mouse). The result is that the individual body ceases to be the point at which there is an intersection, or meeting point, for consciousness and the unconscious. Instead this happens somewhere in cyberspace. The computer screen is both a literal portal and also stands as a metaphor for the interface with the unconscious. Far from positing a digital dualism in which the user is kept separate from the online world, the suggestion is of a blurring of boundaries.

> Individuality is the principle of resistance to collective functioning. It makes possible, and if need be compels, differentiation from the collective psyche...A distinction must be made between *individuality* and the *individual*. The individual is determined on the one hand by the principle of uniqueness and distinctiveness, and on the other by the society to which he belongs. He is an indispensable link in the social structure.[7]

The archetype that provides the framework within which this bridging can take place is termed by Jung the 'persona'. Literally it is the mask worn by an actor in Classic Roman theatre, it is actually more than just a covering. At its most basic and obvious the persona is the mask that is put on through which to face the world. Naturally, every individual has many such masks and one of the first psychological lessons is learning which mask fits which situation. In this sense, the persona is the archetype of social adaptation; it acts as an interface between the personal and the collective. What may appear to be to us our unique and individual way of relating to the world turns out to be the outcome of a collective psychological process. Again, it can be observed that in the technical way we have been using the term, that the persona is an image – a point of contestation and a point of meaning. It is almost like a psychological trace that is placed on the world in an attempt to delineate it and to impose some meaning on it. As Jung comments:

> It is, as its name implies, only a mask of the collective psyche, a mask that *feigns individuality*, making others on oneself believe that one is individual, whereas one is simply acting a role through which the collective psyche speaks. When we analyse the persona we strip off the mask, and discover that what seemed to be individual is at bottom collective; in other worlds, that the persona was only a mask of the collective psyche. Fundamentally the persona is nothing real: it is a compromise between individual and society as to what a man should appear to be.[8]

These shifting persona suggest that playing different roles and adopting different characters is something fundamental, essential even, to the human psyche. It is perhaps unsurprising that when the Web gave the chance to adopt different characters and identities that it proved appealing particularly so as suddenly there was an outlet for fantasy that could bring together like-minded people together without having to leave the comfort of the their real world home. Jung observes that 'Just as we tend to assume the world is as we see it, we naïvely support that people are as we imagine them to be'.[9] The Web, however, is a space where it is explicitly and consciously known that people may not be what they seem. This provides both one of the attractions of the Web and at the very same time gives rise to cultural anxieties about identity theft and imposters with malicious intent. It is a potentially dangerous world, full of shadow fantasies. It provides a way of trying out what it feels like to be someone else, and to gain an insight into how others see us. In psychological terms it potentially offers an opportunity to learn more about ourselves – a chance for greater self-awareness. It also offers the possibility of losing ourselves, of leaving our bodies behind and of living a fantasy.

In this sense, the Web provides a place for the adoption of a new persona or personas. However, the dangers of over identification with the persona must be avoided. The reasons for this have already been hinted at, namely it channels libidinal energy to the object and away from the self, and in so doing the psyche fails to activate the meaning-making function of image formation. The following quote from Jung acts as a summary:

> We must rigorously separate the concept of the individual from that of the persona, for the persona can be entirely dissolved in the collective. But the individual is precisely that which can never be merged with the collective and is never identical with it. That is why identification with the collective and voluntary segregation from it are alike synonymous with disease.[10]

The persona is partly about illusion and is concerned with presenting an image of who we are and what we are like. A more concealed aspect of the psyche is what Jung termed the 'shadow'. Actually the shadow and the persona go hand-in-hand, with the outer image prefiguring the inner one. The shadow is composed from the negative and underdeveloped side of the psyche. It can almost be thought of as the antithesis to the persona. Jung put it concisely noting that it is, 'the thing a person has no wish to be.'[11] Yet it is who we are and if ignored only grows in strength and as it does so it increasingly comes to colour how the world is seen. Unknowingly the shadow is projected on people, objects, relationships and comes to taint them. When there is a disproportional and strong emotional reaction then the level of affect provides a clue that the engagement is one which is partly unconscious. Once again this provides a useful example of how libidinal energy can be channeled away from he self and invested in an alternative relationship.

Perhaps one of the current ways we explore this shadow side to our psyche is in the World Wide Web and it appears to the recipient of a cultural projection as a shadow. Rather than recognize the dark side to our own personalities there is a tendency to project it onto other people and events. Film, television and publishing have all been accused of being corrupting influences and of encouraging violent, disruptive and depraved behaviour. To borrow a phrase from sociology they have been accused as starting 'moral panics'. The attention given to the ageing English pop star Gary Glitter on his release from prison after serving a short sentence for possessing child pornography displays, in part, society's values and moral framework. But another important part of the story which was covered by all the national media in the UK was that the images had been downloaded from the Internet. The Web itself was in someway to blame. It was portrayed as a dangerous and potentially morally corrupt place and something to treat with extreme caution.

The Internet, like the unconscious, is a place we are attracted to but also one of which we can be afraid. Some users want to make the most of its positive qualities and almost at an intuitive level recognize the value of what it has to offer. At the same time others feel a need to censor, deny and demonize its darker side. Such is the fear that institutions and parents, and even some countries, try to impose a filter on the contents of the Internet and protect users. In psychological terms what we have here are the twin processes of projection and repression. The authors of A Critical Dictionary of Jungian Analysis define projection as follows:

> Projection may be seen as normal or pathological and as a defence against anxiety. Difficult emotions and unacceptable parts of the personality may be located in a person or object external to the subject. [12]

Perhaps the interrelatedness of persona and shadow finds some expression via the Internet. The Internet itself is a repository of knowledge and the experiences of humankind, and as such it contains the full gamut of our existence. It should therefore not prove particularly surprising to discover that the persona and the shadow it goes hand-in-hand with are readily experienced on the Net. There is a real sense in which the psychological attitude adopted towards the Net, influence the type of activities and behaviours into which we enter. As Sherry Turkle explains:

> When people adopt an online persona they cross a boundary into highly-charged territory. Some feel an uncomfortable sense of fragmentation, some a sense of relief. Some sense the possibilities for self-discovery, even self-transformation. Serena, a twenty-six-year-old graduate student in history, says, 'When I log on to a new MUD [multi-user dungeon] and I create a character and know I have to start typing my description, I always feel a sense of panic. Like I could find out something I don't want to know.' Arlie, a twenty-year-old undergraduate, says, 'I am always very self-conscious when I create a new character. Usually, I end up creating someone I wouldn't want my parents to know about. It takes me, like, three hours. But that someone is part of me.'[13]

It would be a foolish person who chose to project their shadow onto someone or something that is innocent. Instead what happens is that shadow qualities go unnoticed and the recipient of our projections receives a negative response. Fears and fantasies about the corrosive nature of technology, for example, can also be seen as tainted with such projected material. It is in the denial, or repression, of the shadow which contributes to the negative reaction when it is projected onto others. Repression cannot be a successful strategy because even though the shadow may have been successfully repressed it has not been destroyed. Jung counsels a different course of acting and suggests that the innate drive to self-growth and self-awareness, which he terms 'the individuation process', is so fundamental and strong that we will be forced to acknowledge this dark side to ourselves. What happens is that the shadow grows in strength until the repression mechanisms fail and it eventually invades consciousness. As Jung puts its:

> But if it (the shadow) is repressed and isolated from consciousness, it never gets corrected, and is liable to burst forth suddenly in a moment of unawareness. At all events, it forms an unconscious snag, blocking the most well-meant attempts.[14]

The image of the Web, just like the shadow, is curiously contradictory. It has both good and bad qualities and this doesn't seem quite rational or sensible. This type of ambiguity is a good clue we are dealing with an image that carries some significance for the unconscious – it short it is symbolic. Jung suggests one of the functions of symbols is to hold together apparently contradictory ideas and emotions. 'The symbol is the middle way along which the opposites flow together in a new movement, like a watercourse bringing fertility after a long drought.' [15] If the World Wide Web is indeed a cultural symbol then we are prompted to consider what the opposites are that it might hold together.

The very name World Wide Web conjures up a complex set of culturally confusing and contradictory associations. For users of the Internet, the Web refers to the connected nature of the various computers on the Internet that are used to produce and maintain its websites. But mythologically and culturally webs have a different meaning. They are places of entrapment and labyrinth like – once entered they are difficult to escape from. We also think of the web as an image of deception as in the saying 'What a tangled web we weave when first we practice to deceive'. But in western folklore the spiders' web also has some positive associations: 'Cobweb – The web of a spider is said to have concealed the infant Jesus from Herod's soldiers...destroying a web on purpose will only provoke misfortune...Laying a cobweb on an open wound will promote the healing process.'[16]

As has already been demonstrated, Jung's psychological theories extend beyond the shadow and its associated imagery. One of the helpful aspects of Jung's thought relates to what post-Jungians have termed the 'contrasexual' archetype.[17] Jung suggested that our gendered identities are the result of personal, cultural and historical pressures. His theory of innate psychological patterns noted that there is a state of tension between the innate drive to self-development and the constraints of culture. Jung claimed that irrespective of our biological sex everyone has the capacity to experience the full range of human feelings. For men Jung termed the cultural construction of a feminine identity (as opposed to what it is like to be female) as the *anima*. He posited a similar construct for women in which the traditionally masculine behaviours and attitudes represent themselves in the image of the *animus*. Without getting too involved in the intricacies of this debate what matters is that Jung recognized that everyone has the capacity to explore what culture dictates are male, female, masculine and feminine qualities. Given these psychological propensities, it is not so surprising the opportunities afforded by the Web are used by some to explore alternative gender identities.

Of course, the Net is not the only place where experiments with identity are played out. One important aspect of cinema is it gives the opportunity to adopt transgendered identities and to find a space that in which it is possible to explore the dark and culturally forbidden side of the psyche. In the twilight of the cinema's auditorium it is possible imagine, and to a degree experience, what it is like to be heroine or hero, villain or femme fatale and to let that part of ourselves find some expression. The Web goes one step further and makes it possible to create our own fictional worlds and identities and to explore what it means to live and come to terms with ourselves – however difficult that might be. This could involve exploring the tensions which exist between what it means to be female or feminine, or perhaps to examine the relationship between masculinity and its shadow side that all to easily can manifest itself in aggression and oppression. Whatever we choose, the Web offers us a psychological space within which to surf and interact and where we can play out and examine some of the hidden and repressed parts of our psyche – what is being suggested here is not that in someway the fantasy becomes physical. To argue that would be to confuse the metaphorical images of the inner-world with the concrete nature of the physical world – to adopt a differently gendered identity on the Web is not to change ones gender in the physical world rather, what is being suggested is that the virtual nature of the Web provides a suitably intangible environment in which to explore fantasies about our inner-world.

In thinking about the ambivalent attitude which is culturally adopted towards the Web, the paradox of Buridans's ass comes to mind. A donkey is placed between two equally sized bales of hay. Given that he cannot decide which one to eat the donkey starves to death. Jung' comments on this noting:

> The important thing was not whether the bundle on the right or the one on the left was better, or which one he ought to start eating, but what he wanted in the depths of his being – which did he feel pushed towards? The ass wanted the object to make up his mind for him.[18]

This is the challenge of analytical psychology – to make up our own minds to live the life we want and not just to react to the pressures of life, real enough though they are. The concept of projection reveals some of the contradictory ways in which the Web is culturally positioned.

In analytical psychology the process of discriminating between what is real in a situation and what is the result of unconscious psychological drives involves 'dissolving' projection. Never an easy undertaking but the process is made ever more difficult because from a psychological vantage point those that espouse the moral dangers of the Internet have a point. For example, there is no defense for the exploitation of children in pornography, although paedophiles will have their own reasons and justification for their behaviour. The reality is that such material forms a tiny part of what is on the Web, but what it carries with it is disproportionate affect. The issue is how to separate out the fear and fantasy from the reality. In working psychologically it is possible to acknowledge the contradictory views that are held towards the Web. Psychological development is about understanding the oppositions and tensions which exist within ourselves and how that affects the way we relate to our culture. Using analytical psychology in this manner directs us away from particular instances of Web use and instead directs us to consider the cultural responses which are made to the Web. This tells us about both the use to which the Net is put but more importantly it helps us to identify and understand some of our culturally repressed psychological fears and fantasies.

This is entirely consistent and congruent with a Jungian view about psychotherapy and analysis. From this perspective, analysis is as much about an attitude towards life as it is a clinical process. The activities of introspection, of clarity in thinking, of opening up choices are all equally part of living a psychological life. Perhaps, most importantly, therapy will not make the problems of life disappear. Problems, obstacles, challenges, call them what you will, are not only unavoidable they are, in fact, an indispensable part of life. What a therapeutic approach to life can offer is a means through which to understand the relationships we have both with our inner-life and with our relationships in the world.

Equally, analytical psychology offers a way in which to think about how the Internet is used. It offers a framework within which to reflect on why it has developed in the manner in which it has and why it is both valued and feared. The central role of the image as a meaning-making function in the psyche leads straight to the importance of fantasy in everyday life. Without question, the World Wide Web is certainly a realm of fantasy which contains an outpouring of desire alongside the opportunity to act on it. In a psychology sense it offers a new opportunity to explore who we are and what we might become.

Notes

1. Jung, C. G. (1953/66) *Collected Works* vol. 7. (London: Routledge and Kegan Paul), para. 490. Emphasis as original.
2. *Ibid.*, para. 504.
3. *Ibid.*, para. 486.
4. Jung, C. G. (1960/69) *Collected Works* vol. 8. (London: Routledge and Kegan Paul), para. 523.
5. Jung, C. G. (1955/70) *Collected Works* vol. 14. (London: Routledge and Kegan Paul), para. 206.
6. Jung, C. G. (1953/66) *Collected Works* vol. 7. (London: Routledge and Kegan Paul), para. 507. Emphasis as original.
7. *Ibid.*, para. 519. Emphasis as original.
8. *Ibid.*, para. 245–6. Emphasis as original.
9. Jung, C. G. (1960/69) *Collected Works* vol. 8. (London: Routledge and Kegan Paul), para. 507.
10. Jung, C. G. (1953/66) *Collected Works* vol. 7. (London: Routledge and Kegan Paul), para. 485. Emphasis as original.
11. Jung, C. G. (1954/66) *Collected Works* vol. 16. (London: Routledge and Kegan Paul), para. 470.

12. Samuels, A. *et al.*, *A Critical Dictionary of Jungian Analysis.* (London: Routledge Kegan Paul), p. 113.
13. Turkle, S. *Life on Screen: Identity in the Age of the Internet.* (Orion Books: London, 1997), p. 260.
14. Jung, C. G. (1958/69) *Collected Works* vol. 11. (London: Routledge and Kegan Paul), para. 131.
15. Jung, C. G. (1964/71) *Collected Works* vol. 6. (London: Routledge and Kegan Paul), para, 433.
16. Pickering, A. *Dictionary of Superstitions* (London: Cassell, 1995), pp. 244–5.
17. c.f. Samuels. A., *Jung and the Post-Jungians.* (London: Routledge 1985),
18. Jung, C. G. (1953/66) *Collected Works* vol. 7. (London: Routledge and Kegan Paul), para. 487.

CONCLUSION

This book has clearly adopted a psychological stance in its reflections on contemporary mediated communication. In fact, it has attempted slightly more than this suggests. In looking at how audiences and viewers use television, cinema and the Internet, it has been trying to take a fresh look at some of the issues raised by audio-visual mediated communication. As this complex and often unconscious relationship has been teased out, the intention has been to reposition how the media are seen. In focusing on why images have meanings that are not immediately apparent, *Frames of Mind* has been engaging in a quasi-therapeutic activity.

It therefore follows that underpinning this book is the project of taking analysis out of the consulting room and relocating it in the wider worlds of society and culture at large. Clearly, analysis, or therapy, is not the same as reading a book, no one would claim that it is; for therapy is an experience whose roots lie firmly, and deeply, in the relationship between two people. But there is something in the Jungian approach whether it is applied in understanding relationships or other creative forms such as literature, film, art, television, the Internet and such like that encourages a change in the mindset of the person undertaking the enquiry. Indeed, it is not going too far to say that it requires such a change. In psychotherapy both the client and the therapist change as a result of their encounter. So too in working with images in a post-Jungian manner it is hard, if not impossible, for the individual undertaking that work not also to be altered. Jung suggests as much:

> Analysis, thus understood, is by no means a therapeutic method of which the medical profession holds a monopoly. It is an art, a technique, a science of psychological life, which the patient, when cured, should continue to practise for his own good and for the good of those amongst whom he lives. If he understands it in this way, he will not set himself up as a prophet, nor as a world reformer; but, with a sound sense of the general good, he will profit by the knowledge he as acquired during treatment, and his influence will make itself felt more by the example of his own life than by any high discourse or missionary propaganda.[1]

Ironically, in suggesting the avoidance of high-discourse and missionary propaganda Jung adopts a more than slightly evangelical tone. In many ways this is unfortunate as, at its very core, analytical psychology does not offer a self-help or fast-track route to perfection. It is not about a quasi-religious route to salvation nor, arguably, does it aim to cure or even promote mental health. What certainly is of central concern to analytical psychology is wholeness and the aim of Jungian psychology is to help individuals become wholly who they are and to live a full life in accord with that sense of themselves. In an image-saturated world the media, whether they are invited or not, form a significant part of that life. To ignore their role in a psychology of the self would be an act of repression and denial.

The challenge here is twofold. The first and most obvious challenge posed by this book is for media academics to take seriously the insights that a post-Jungian therapeutic approach has to offer. There are many reasons why this is difficult. Jungian ideas are not widely known and are frequently misunderstood. Sometimes issues around Jung's personal life prove too high a stumbling block and consequently make his clinical and theoretical insights inaccessible. Even so, Jungian studies is currently flourishing and presently there is an ever burgeoning body of scholarly writing provided by academics and analysts alike for anyone with an interest in this field. The second challenge is for clinicians to welcome the mediated world, which is so much part of the lives of their clients, into the consulting room. In psychotherapy trainings, images are talked about and in some detail. But the only perspective offered is the one of the clinical orientation which is being taught. The work of academics who engage with cultural, film and media theory is not widely known and is largely left unmentioned. This is a lost opportunity as the two have much to offer each other.

All this said, it is not that analytical psychology can, in and of itself, provide answers to the role, function or use that might be made of contemporary mediated communications. However, what it does offer is a way of re-conceptualizing the attitude that as individuals we adopt to the media. It also provides productive means by which to reflect on the relationship that exists between the values and attitudes of society and the images it produces and watches.

As has been stressed at numerous points throughout this book, of course images tell us something. Superficially this is at the level of iconic representation – images look like objects in the physical world and it is possible to reflect on why this or that image might be important, or indeed not. But of more significance are the intangible affects that become attached to images. While the iconic serves to activate such a response it is at the deeper, more metaphorical, levels of the psyche that the affect drives us towards making meaning. If nothing else, analytical psychology can help to understand the psychological meanings which arise as a result of the interaction between image and viewer and, hence, between media and society.

This suggests an avenue for future research. Each chapter in this book has given a view of a particular subject. Sometimes this has been somewhat theoretical, as in the discussions around affect. At other points the approach as been more applied, for example, in the analyses of *Chinatown* and television advertising. Hopefully, the cumulative effect of this has been to gradually build up a picture of how analytical psychology can be used to analyse the media. Inevitably the process has raised as many issues as it has resolved. In considering the psychological status of 'the image' it is still uncertain whether it is possible to preserve the specificity of each medium (television, film, the Internet etc.) while at the same time adopting a consistently post-Jungian approach. There is also the undoubted tension that exists between images as they appear on the screen, and the more therapeutic understanding of 'image' as something which encapsulates the reality and meaning of an individual's emotional and intellectual response. Finally, there is also a tension and interaction between the meanings which individuals create and the meanings society collectively finds in the products of the mass media.

The question as to whether there can ever be a unified psychotherapeutic theory of the screen is quite clearly not one which can be answered here. Nor, at this point, is it even possible to know if such a unified theory is desirable. However, it is the case that post-Jungian theory has helped to seek out new problems, questions and tensions. As mentioned earlier, post-Jungian psychology is not about providing answers and it is quite probable that images, because they encapsulate the complexity of the relationship between consciousness and the unconscious, will ultimately remain ethereal and unknowable.

Note
1. Jung, C. G, (1953/66) *Collected Works* vol. 7. (London: Routledge and Kegan Paul), para. 502.

BIBLIOGRAPHY

Adams, M. A., *The Mythological Unconscious*. (Karnac: London, 2001).

Alvarado, M., and Thompson, R., *The Media Reader*. (British Film Institute: London, 1990).

Andreadis, A., *To Seek Out New Life: The Biology of Star Trek*. (Crown Publishers: New York, 1998).

Barrett, M., and Barrett, D., *Star Trek: The Human Frontier*. (Polity: Cambridge, 2001).

Barthes, R., *Image, Music, Text*. Trans Heath, S. (Fontana; London, 1977).

Bergstrom, J., (ed.), *Endless Night: Cinema and Psychoanalysis, Parallel Histories*. (University of California Press: Berkeley and Los Angeles, 1999).

Campbell, J., *The Hero with a Thousand Faces*. Princeton University Press: Princeton, 1949.

Casement, A., *Carl Gustav Jung*. Sage: London, 2001.

Clancey, K. and Krieg, P., *Counter Intuitive Marketing: Achieve Great Results using Uncommon Sense*, (The Free Press: New York, 2000).

Chrétien de Troyes, *Arthurian Romances: Perceval*, trans. Owen, D. R. (Dent and Sons, Guernsey, 1987).

Dyer, G., *Advertising as Communication*. (Routledge: London, 1982).

Dickason, R. *British Television Advertising: Cultural Identity and Communication*. (University of Luton Press: Luton, 2000).

Eaton, M., *Chinatown*. (British Film Institute: London, 1997).

Ellis, J., *Visible Fictions: Cinema, Television, Video*. (Routledge: London, 1982).

Fern, Y., *Inside the Mind of Gene Roddenberry The Creator of Star Trek*. (HarperCollins: London, 1995).

Gabbard, G., *Psychodynamic Psychiatry in Clinical Practice: The DSM IV Edition*. (American Psychiatric Press: Washington, 1994).

Gauntlett, D., and Hill, A., *TV Living: Television, Culture and Everyday Life*. (British Film Institute: London, 1999).

Gennep, A., *The Rite of Passage*. (Routledge and Kegan Paul: London, 1960).

Glenn Frank, quoted in Williams, R., *The Wizard of Ads: Turning Words into Magic and Dreams*. (Bard Press: Austin Texas, 1998).

Goethals, G., *The TV Ritual: Worshiping at the Video Altar*. (Beacon Press Books: Boston, 1981).

Gray, C. (eds), *The Cyborg Handbook*. (Routledge: London, 1995).

Gregory, C., *Star Trek Parallel Narratives*. (Macmillan: London, 2000).

Hanley, R., *The Metaphysics of Star Trek*. (Basic Books: New York, 1977).

Hanna, B., *Encounters with the Soul: Active Imagination as Developed by C. G. Jung*. (Cambridge: Sigo Press, 1981).

Harrison, T. et al. (eds), *Enterprise Zones: Critical Positions on Star Trek*. Eds Harrison et al. (Westview Press: Boulder, 1996).

Hastie, A., *Fabricated Space: Assimilating the Individual on Star Trek: The Next Generation*, in *Enterprise Zones: Critical Positions on Star Trek*. Eds Harrison et al. (Westview Press: Boulder, 1996).

Hauke, C., *Jung and the Postmodern: The Interpretation of Realities*. (Routledge; London: 2000).

Haynes, J., and Shearer, A. (eds), *When a Princess Dies: Reflections from Jungian Analysts*. (London: Harvest, 1998).

Herbert, G., *Teach me my God and King*, source Hymns and Psalms: A Methodist and Ecumenical Hymn Book. (The Methodist Publishing House: London, 1983).

Hillman, J., *Emotion: A Comprehensive Phenomenology of Theories and Their Meanings for Therapy*. (Routledge and Kegan Paul: London, 1960).

Hillman, J., *Re-Visioning Psychology*. (Harper and Row: New York, 1977).

Hillman, J., *The Dream and the Underworld*. (Harper and Row: New York, 1979).

Holmyard, J., *Alchemy*. (Penguin Books: Harmondsworth, 1957).

Holy Bible, *New Revised Standard Version: Anglicized Edition with Apocrypha*. (Oxford University Press: Oxford, 1975).

Homans P., *Jung in Context: Modernity and the Making of a Psychology*. (University of Chicago Press: Chicago, 1979).

Izod, J., *Myth, Mind and the Screen: Understanding the Heroes of Our Time*. (Cambridge University Press: Cambridge, 2001).

Izod, J., *Screen, Culture, Psyche. A Post-Jungian Approach to Working with the Audience*. (Routledge: London, 2006).

Jacoby, M., *Individuation and Narcissism: The Psychology of Self in Jung and Kohut*. (Routledge: London, 1990).

Jenson, R., *The Dream Society: How the Coming Shift from Information to Imagination will Transform your Business*. (McGraw-Hill: New York, 1999).

Jung, C. G., *Collected Works of C. G. Jung*, edited, Read, H., Fordham, M., Adler, G., translated by Hull, R., (Routledge: London).

Vol. 1.

1. *Psychiatric Studies*, (1957, 1970)
2. *Experimental Researches*, (1973)
3. *The Psychogenesis of Mental Disease*, (1960)
4. *Freud and Psychoanalysis*, (1961)
5. *Symbols of Transformation*, (1956, 1967)
6. *Psychological Types*, (1921)
7. *Two Essays on Analytical Psychology*, (1953, 1966)
8. *The Structure and Dynamics of the Psyche*, (1960, 1969)

9.I.   *The Archetypes and the Collective Unconscious*, (1959)
9.II. *Aion*, (1951)
10.   *Civilisation in Transition*, (1964)
11.   *Psychology and Religion: West and East*, (1958, 1969)
12.   *Psychology and Alchemy*, (1944)
13.   *Alchemical Studies*, (1967)
14.   *Mysterium Coniunctionis*, (1963, 1970)
15.   *The Spirit in Man, Art and Literature*, (1966)
16.   *The Practice of Psychotherapy*, (1954, 1966)
17.   *The Development of Personality*, (1954)
18.   *The Symbolic Life*, (1977)
19.   *Bibliography of C. G. Jung's Writings*
20.   *General Index to the Collected Works*

Supplementary Vol. A. *The Zofingia Lectures*, edited
McGuire, W., (London, 1983).

Seminar Papers, Part 1. *Dream Analysis: Notes of the Seminar given in 1928–30*, edited
McGuire, W., (London, 1984).
Visions: Notes of the Seminar Given in 1930–34 vols 1 & 2 ed. Douglas, C.

Jung, C. G., *Modern Man in Search of a Soul*. Trans. Dell, W. S. and Baynes, C. F. (London,
    1985).
Jung, C. G., *Memories, Dreams, Reflections*. (Flamingo: London, 1963).
Jung, C. G., (editor), *Man and his Symbols*. (Picador: London, 1964).
Jung, C. G., *Letters*. (Princeton: University of Princeton Press, 1973).
Jung, C. G. and Freud, S., *The Freud/Jung Letters*. (Picador: London, 1974. This edition,
    London, 1979).
Jung, C. G., *C. G. Jung Speaking: Interviews and Encounters*. Ed. McGuire, W. and Hull,
    R. F. C. (Picador: London, 1980).
Kohut, H., *The Analysis of Self*. (International Universities Press: New York: 1971).
Kohut, H., *The Restoration of Self*. (International Universities Press: New York: 1977).
Krauss, L., *The Physics of Star Trek*. (Harper Collins: London, 1995).
Laplance, J. and Pontalis J. B., *The Language of Psycho-Analysis*. Trans. Nicolson-Smith,
    D., (Karnac Books: London, 1988).
Lévi-Strauss, C., *The Raw and the Cooked: Introduction to a Science of Mythology*.
    (Random House: London, 1969).
Longinotti-Buitoni, L. G. with Longinotti-Buitoni, K., *Selling Dreams: How to Make Any
    Product Irresistible*. (Simon and Schuster: New York, 1999).
Masterman, L., *Cul-de-sac: Through the Mirror of Surrealism*. Screen: The Journal of the
    Society for Education in Film and Television. Vol 11. Number 9, pp. 44–60.
Mayne, J., *Cinema and Spectatorship*. (Routledge: London, 1993).
McLuhan, M., *Understanding Media: The Extensions of Man*. (Massachusetts Institute of
    Technology Press, Cambridge: Massachusetts, 1995).
Metz, C., *Psychoanalysis and Cinema: The Imaginary Signifier*. Trans. Britton, C.,
    Williams, A., Brester, B. and Guzzetti, A. eds., Heath, S. and MacCabe, C. (Macmillan
    Press: London, 1982).

Myers, K., *Understains.* (Comedia: London, 1986).

Nagy, M., *Philosophical Issues in the Psychology of C. G. Jung.* (State University of New York Press: Albany, 1991).

Noll, R., *The Jung Cult: Origins of a Charismatic Movement.* (Princeton University Press: Princeton, 1994).

Noll, R., *The Aryan Christ: The Secret Life of Carl Gustav Jung.* (Macmillan: London, 1997).

Okuda, M. and Okuda, D. with Mirek, D., *The Star Trek Encyclopaedia: A Reference Guide to the Future.* (Pocket Books: New York).

Ovid, *The Metamorphoses of Ovid.* Trans. Mary M. Innes, (Penguin: Harmondsworth, 1955).

Papadopoulos, R. & Saayman, G., *Jung in Modern Perspective.* (Wildwood House ltd, Hounslow, 1984).

Propp, V., *Morphology of the Folktale.* (University of Texas Press: Austin, 1975).

Projansky, S., *When the Body Speaks,* in *Enterprise Zones: Critical Positions on Star Trek.* Eds Harrison *et al.* (Westview Press: Boulder, 1996).

Richards, T., *The Meaning of Star Trek.* (Doubleday: New York, 1997).

Roth, P., *The Human Stain.* (Jonathan Cape: London, 2000).

Rowland, S., *Jung as a Writer.* (London: Routledge, 2005).

Saito, A., *Hitchcock's Trilogy: A Logic of Mise en Scène.* In Bergstrom, J., ed., *Endless Night: Cinema and Psychoanalysis, Parallel Histories.* (University of California Press: Berkeley and Los Angeles: 1999).

Samuels, A., *Jung and the Post-Jungians.* (Routledge: London, 1985).

Samuels, A., The Political Psyche. (Routledge: London, 1993).

Samules, A., *Politics on the Couch: Citizenship and the Internal Life.* (Profile Books: London, 2001).

Schiller, H., *Information Inequality: The Deepening Social Crisis in America.* (Routledge: London, 1996).

Schore, A., *Affect Dysregulation and Disorders of the Self.* W. W. Norton and Company: London, 2003.

Schwartz-Salant, N., *Narcissism and Character Transformation: The Psychology of Narcissistic Character Disorders.* (Inner City Books: Toronto, 1982).

Shamdasani, S., *Cult Fictions: C.G. Jung and the Founding of Analytical Psychology.* (Routledge: London, 1998).

Springer, C., *Electronic Eros: Bodies and Desire in the Postindustrial Age.* University of Texas Press: Austin, 1996.

Turkle, S., *Life on Screen: Identity in the Age of the Internet.* (Orion Books: London, 1997).

Valentinus, B., *The Practica, with Twelve Keys, and an Appendix Thereto, Concerning the Great Stone of the Ancient Sage.* In Waite, 1893.

Vinge, L., *The Narcissus Theme in Western Literature up to the Early Nineteenth Century.* Trans. R. Dewsnap. (Gleerups: Lund, 1967).

Waddell, T., *Mis/takes: Archetype, Myth and Identity in Screen Fiction.* (Routledge: London, 2006).

Waite, A., *The Hermetic Museum.* (London, 1893).

Wess, R., and Ross, B. *Make it so: Leadership Lessons from Star Trek: The Next Generation*. (Pocket Books: New York, 1996).

Wilkinson, M., *Coming into Mind: The Mind-Brain Relationship, a Clinical Jungian Perspective*. Routledge: London, 2006.

Williams, R., *Television: Technology and Cultural Form*. (Schocken Books: London, 1975).

Williams, R., 'Advertising: the Magic System' in *Problems in Materialism and Culture*, (London: Verso, 1980).

Williams, R., *Secret Formulas of the Wizard of Ads*. (Bard Press: Austin Texas, 1999).

Williams, R., *The Wizard of Ads: Turning Words into Magic and Dreams*. (Bard Press: Austin Texas, 1998).

Williamson, J., *Decoding Advertisements: Ideology and Meaning in Advertising*. (Marion Boyars: London, 1978).

INDEX